Welcome to
What if...
Book of Alternative
Military History

The stories we encounter as we explore history are captivating. However, one irresistible question we are often left with is, "What if it happened differently?" In this new volume of *What if... Book of Alternative Military History*, experts examine defining moments in battles, wars and conflicts through the ages and across the globe, and paint a picture of how things could have gone. We will ask, "What if the USA had won the Vietnam War?" We'll explore an alternate reality where Pompey defeated Julius Caesar, and look at what would have happened if Boudicca's revolution had succeeded. All this and more can be found when you turn the page.

Contents

6 What if... the Confederacy had won at Antietam?

10 What if... the USA had launched an invasion of Canada?

14 What if... Napoleon had won at Trafalgar?

18 What if... Argentina had won the Falklands War?

22 What if... Operation Valkyrie had assassinated Hitler?

26 What if... the USA had won the Vietnam War?

30 What if... the USSR had invented the atomic bomb first?

34 What if... Philip II had lost the Battle of Chaeronea?

38 What if... the Dunkirk evacuation had failed?

42 What if... Pompey had defeated Julius Caesar?

46 What if... the Franks had lost the Battle of Tours?

50 What if... the Spanish Empire had tried to invade China?

54 What if... the RAF had lost the Battle of Britain?

58 What if... Joan of Arc hadn't broken the Siege of Orleans?

62 What if... South America had joined World War I?

66 What if... Boudicca's revolution had succeeded?

70 What if... Able Archer 83 had turned to war?

74 What if... Suleiman I had seized Vienna?

78 What if... Japan had refused to surrender?

82 What if... the Chinese communists had lost?

86 What if... Mexico had defeated the United States?

6

34

102

90 What if… the First Crusade had been defeated?

94 What if… Britain had not won the Seven Years' War?

98 What if… Germany had won WWI?

102 What if… Stalingrad had fallen to the Nazis?

106 What if… the Persians had conquered the Greeks?

110 What if… US forces had retreated from Korea?

114 What if… Napoleon had won the Battle of Waterloo?

118 What if… Britain had won the War of Independence?

122 What if… Entente had forced a win in Gallipoli?

126 What if… the US had stayed out of the Great War?

What if...

THE CONFEDERACY HAD WON AT ANTIETAM?

Confederate victory at Antietam might have contributed to the end of Abraham Lincoln's presidency in the election of 1864

INTERVIEW WITH

Dr Gary W Gallagher

Dr Gallagher is the John L Nau III Professor in the History of the American Civil War, Emeritus, at the Corcoran Department of History, University of Virginia. He received his Bachelor of Arts degree at Adams State College in 1972 and Master of Arts and Doctorate at the University of Texas, Austin, in 1977 and 1982. Dr Gallagher is the author or co-author of numerous books, essays and published lectures, receiving many awards and accolades as one of the preeminent Civil War historians of our time.

RIGHT
General Robert E Lee led the Confederate Army into Maryland in 1862

General Robert E Lee's Confederate Army of Northern Virginia was turned back during the Battle of Antietam, its first invasion of the North during the American Civil War (1861-65). General George B McClellan, commanding the Union Army of the Potomac, claimed victory but has been criticised for failing to win decisively. Still, Antietam was a turning point in the war. In its aftermath, President Abraham Lincoln issued the Emancipation Proclamation, support for recognition of the Confederacy and even direct intervention by Great Britain was quelled, and Lee's wounded army retired to the safety of Virginia. How would a Confederate victory at Antietam have impacted the Lincoln presidency and the course of the Civil War?

How would a Confederate victory at the Battle of Antietam have affected the presidency of Abraham Lincoln?
The late summer of 1862 was a very difficult time for Lincoln and the Union. The terrible fighting of the Seven Days and then the defeat at Second Bull Run had put Lincoln in a rough place. The off-year elections were looming, and the ability to retain control of the government was always linked to how the armies were doing in the field. The House of Representatives and the Senate included many Democrats, and Democrat voters made up about 45 percent of the electorate.

To move forward on emancipation, Lincoln needed broad support, and he not only needed Republicans in the army but Democrats as well. The ante was upped considerably when the most famous Rebel army crossed the Potomac River into the United States. A Union defeat at Antietam would not have been good for the Lincoln administration, that's for sure. It would have complicated Lincoln's life tremendously. It would have deferred the Emancipation Proclamation at least for a short time, pushing that down the road until what at least appeared to be a victory had occurred. I don't know if the victory at Stones River in Tennessee in the Western theatre at the end of the year would have been enough.

Lincoln would not have resigned. He had two more years before he had to run again, and things can shift so quickly and dramatically in wartime. Look at the summer of 1864: it was the darkest time of the war, and it appeared as though he would not be re-elected. He issued the famous Blind Memorandum that stated as much and that the war would have to be won before the Democrats took over since they would not be in a position to win after they had taken the White House. Then General [William] Sherman took Atlanta and General [Philip] Sheridan won victories in the Shenandoah Valley. That turned things around completely, and when things shift on the battlefield, then morale shifts behind the lines.

What would have happened to Lincoln if he had not been re-elected in 1864? Would he have survived?
He would have become a one-term president who'd failed, who had presided over a failed war effort. A lot of things had to click into place for his assassination to have occurred. I think Lincoln would have had to be re-elected for his assassination to take place. I do take John Wilkes Booth at his word as he said he was in the audience when Lincoln gave a speech stating that Black men would be given the right to vote. That was it for Booth. He could not stand the thought of Black men voting.

Lincoln won the election of 1864 because Atlanta fell to Sherman's Union army and because of Sheridan's Valley campaign with the victory at the Third Battle of Winchester. These occurred between the first and third weeks of September, and then Sheridan won another victory at Cedar Creek in October. These were huge victories, and that is the elephant in the room. If Sherman and Sheridan had not won on the battlefield, Lincoln would have lost the election of 1864, maybe not to George McClellan, but

What if... THE CONFEDERACY HAD WON AT ANTIETAM?

THE PAST

1862
MCCLELLAN SQUANDERS OPPORTUNITY

General George B McClellan's Union Army of the Potomac substantially outnumbered General Robert E Lee's Confederate Army of Northern Virginia during the Maryland Campaign, but even the discovery of Lee's Special Order No 191 failed to spur McClellan to decisive action. The order, found in a camp recently occupied by Confederate troops, outlined Lee's entire plan for the campaign. When he read it, McClellan shouted: "Here is a paper with which, if I cannot whip Bobby Lee, I will be willing to go home." Still, McClellan was slow in his pursuit of Lee and committed his troops piecemeal during Antietam, which resulted in a tactical draw but enough of a strategic Union victory to compel Lee to withdraw into Virginia.

1863
LINCOLN ISSUES EMANCIPATION PROCLAMATION

On 22 September 1862, Lincoln issued a preliminary proclamation. The final version of the Emancipation Proclamation was signed on 1 January 1863, and declared that "all persons held as slaves" in states then in rebellion against the US "are, and henceforward shall be free". The proclamation did little to change the circumstances of slaves in territory not under the control of the Union army, but the character of the Civil War changed in that the abolition of slavery became a declared war aim of the US.

1864
AFTER WINNING REELECTION, LINCOLN IS ASSASSINATED

Lincoln defeated McClellan in the November election, 212-21 votes in the electoral college. "Lincoln was lucky that he had his best commanders come forward when they did," explains Dr Gary W Gallagher. "He was fortunate to have General [Ulysses S] Grant, and that partnership was key." In winning another presidential term, Lincoln sealed his own fate and was assassinated by John Wilkes Booth in April 1865, just weeks after delivering his second inaugural address.

ABOVE
Union troops charge Confederates at the Battle of Antietam

BELOW
George B McClellan commanded the Army of the Potomac at Antietam

to some Democrat. And this is despite the fact that a Confederate force under General Jubal Early had threatened Washington, DC, in June 1864 and actually lobbed a few artillery shells into the city.

During his second inaugural address, Lincoln acknowledged the significance of the fact that the Union was winning the war when he said: "The progress of our arms, upon which all else chiefly depends..." To me, anyone trying to figure out why this or that might have happened must always look at what the armies were doing. Trying to craft a narrative that doesn't involve the military situation is so wrong-headed.

How would the Union war effort have been affected in the immediate aftermath of a Confederate victory at the Battle of Antietam?
General McClellan would have hunkered down and stayed close to Washington, and a Union defeat at Antietam would have brought into even sharper relief that someone had to rise up to command the US armies in the Eastern Theatre of the war. Lincoln could not just put a sign up that read: 'Capable Army Commander Please Come In.' I don't think a Union defeat at Antietam would have lost the war, but I do think it would have complicated Lincoln's life quite a bit.

Aside from delaying the Emancipation Proclamation, how would a Confederate victory at Antietam have impacted the cause of emancipation?
Emancipation was tied directly to what the soldiers were doing. Wherever the US armies went, there was a chance for emancipation. Juneteenth occurred in Texas in 1865, and that was because emancipation didn't come to Texas until 1865. The Union army didn't get to Texas until that time. Generals like Sherman didn't particularly care about Black people, but the army was the

> "Lee's army was in horrible condition"

ABOVE LEFT Lincoln issued the Emancipation Proclamation after victory at Antietam

ABOVE RIGHT A crowd gathers in Washington, DC, for Lincoln's second inaugural address

engine of emancipation during the Civil War just like the British Army had been during the War of 1812 and the American Revolution.

Would Great Britain have become involved in the American Civil War with a Confederate victory at Antietam?
British Prime Minister Lord Palmerston and the Foreign Secretary John Russell had already discussed the possibility that Britain might attempt to broker a deal that would bring the war to an end. A Confederate victory at Antietam would have certainly brought some kind of reaction from London. It would not necessarily have involved sending troops to support the Confederacy, but who knows exactly what it would have been? Regardless, it would not have been good for Lincoln or for the United States.

Why didn't the people of Maryland rally to the Confederate cause as Lee had hoped?
The Army of Northern Virginia was in the wrong part of Maryland, the Unionist part and the part that did not have many slaveholders. Lee's army was in horrible condition in the autumn of 1862, and only a general with Lee's audacity would have taken that army into the United States, crossing the Potomac River.

Lee's army was ragged and in its worst shape until late in the war, but he wanted to give respite to the farmers of northern Virginia and provide them an opportunity to bring in their harvest, while he supplied his army in Maryland and the northern part of the Valley. Lee knew he was outnumbered and felt that the best tactic was to make his opponent conform to what he was doing. He has been criticised for that, but I think he was right. The Army of Northern Virginia was played out logistically. Lee needed to give that respite to the people of northern Virginia and to replenish his army as well.

What would have been the next military move of Lee and the Confederate Army of Northern Virginia following a victory at the Battle of Antietam?
Lee's army was really small in September and October, with about 50,000 men and with only about 35,000 present at Antietam, and it haemorrhaged [men]. McClellan had 85,000 men, so there were real limits to what Lee could accomplish at Antietam, and the relative proximity of the two armies to logistical support was easier for McClellan.

Lee was not in a position to threaten Washington, DC, or Philadelphia so I believe he would have tried to remain in the North as long as possible, manoeuvring through the rich agricultural part of Maryland and possibly defending the passes in South Mountain, while knowing that every day he was on US soil would cause problems for the Lincoln administration. His presence there would also help the Democratic party's opposition to Lincoln, and that was good for the Confederacy.

If you swap commanders at Antietam, I believe Lee would have been the victor. McClellan failed to use his numerical superiority – some of the Union troops were not even engaged in the fighting at Antietam. After the battle, Lee stayed on the field for a full day and then withdrew across the Potomac in one night. It took McClellan seven weeks to cross the river.

THE POSSIBILITY

1862
MARYLANDERS SUPPORT THE CONFEDERACY
General Robert E Lee believed that a victory on Union soil might yield immense benefits for the Confederacy, including the support of Marylanders. Recruits, he hoped, would rally to the cause and augment the ranks of his battle-worn Army of Northern Virginia. Maryland farmers would contribute to the sustenance of the Confederate forces, and Virginia farmers gather their harvests amid a temporary peace. While Marylanders were initially reluctant, a Confederate victory at Antietam might have led to Maryland seceding from the Union and joining the Confederacy.

1863
GREAT BRITAIN INTERVENES
The British government weighed the advantages and risks associated with involvement, diplomatic and/or military, in the American conflict. The British textile industry depended on the availability of Confederate cotton, but direct intervention might mean war with the US. A Confederate victory at Antietam, which followed the battlefield success at Second Bull Run, might have brought Britain closer to direct support of the Rebel cause, perhaps even with a commitment of naval and land forces.

1864
LINCOLN EXITS, DEMOCRATS NEGOTIATE PEACE
A Confederate victory at Antietam could have led to the eventual end of Lincoln's political career and decreased the probability of his assassination. Assuming he gained the Republican nomination for a second term in 1864, continuing battlefield defeats would have meant the Democratic challenger in the presidential election would likely have won the White House. A Confederate victory would likely have ended General McClellan's military and political careers too. He had stated his intent to see the war through to Union victory, denying his party platform's peace plank. The end of McClellan's ambitions would have paved the way for another Democrat to take centre stage and negotiate an end to the Civil War.

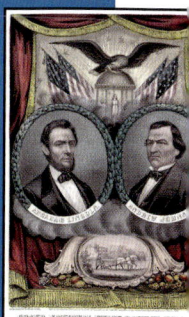

What if...

THE USA HAD LAUNCHED AN INVASION OF CANADA?

If War Plan Red had gone ahead, American troops would have marched on British imperial interests in North America and the Atlantic

INTERVIEW WITH

Graham M Simons

One of the founders of the aviation museum near Duxford, Cambridge, Graham M Simons has written books such as *Boeing 707 Group: A History* and *Howard Hughes And The Spruce Goose*. *The Secret US Plan To Overthrow The British Empire* discusses War Plan Red within a wider context of a US-initiated regime change.

What was War Plan Red?
War Plan Red was one of a myriad of plans and schemes that got developed by the US War Department in the late 1920s. There was War Plan Red, which was the destruction of the British Empire, but there were other colours that involved changing the regimes in Japan, Africa and many of the European countries. When carrying out my research, I found two copies of the actual documentation and followed it right away through from there. I think this accidentally got declassified, as I explain in my book. I stumbled across the entire War Plan Red thing primarily by accident.

Can you briefly outline the plan?
The basic concept of it was that America invaded the Caribbean and Canada. That would force a reaction from the British Empire that would bring out the Royal Navy, which the US Navy would be prepared to attack and destroy. If they destroyed the Royal Navy, that would remove the British Empire's links and protection around the world. In the 1930s we had commercial links down through the Horn of Africa and around the Cape. The British even had commercial roots out to the Far East and to Australia and New Zealand. If you destroy the Royal Navy it removes the protection to these areas.

That would severely reduce the influence of the British Empire and the countries of the Empire. America would then pick up that influence. It was an invasion of Canada, going north, but it was also the invasion of British territories in the Caribbean, purely to protect American access to the Panama Canal. It was also through Canada to protect the Pacific side, certainly the American northwest. The port of Vancouver in Canada had easy access to Alaska in the far north, and then down the northwest, as far south as San Francisco in California. So there are two ways of looking at it: it was going north in one direction and south in the other to protect American interests in the Panama region.

How did the plan come about?
After World War I, the horrors of that conflict brought campaigns for peace, but at the same time there was a certain feeling that America should consider itself first. Within the American political

RIGHT
War Plan Red would have seen US troops storming the Canadian border

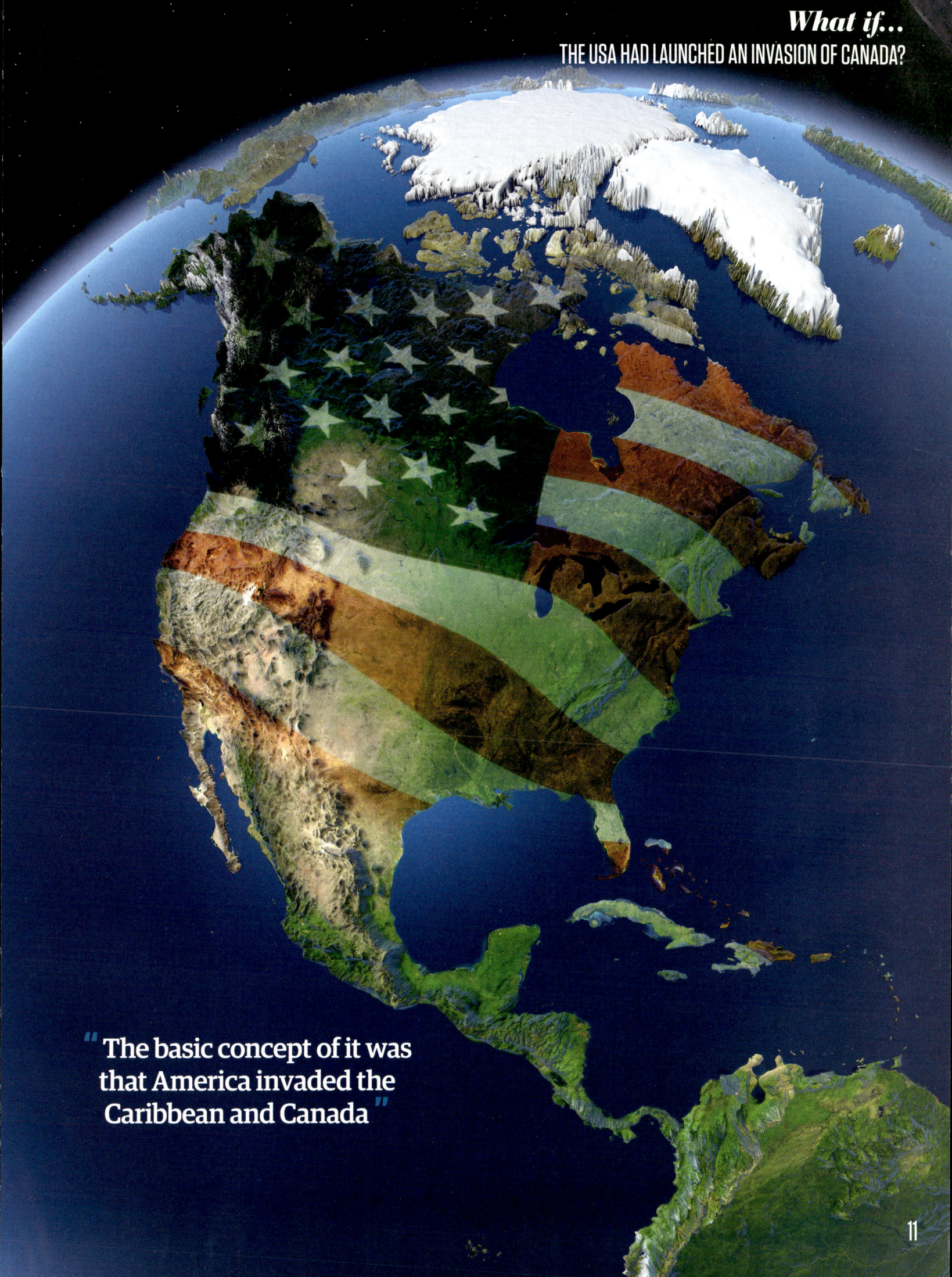

What if...
THE USA HAD LAUNCHED AN INVASION OF CANADA?

" The basic concept of it was that America invaded the Caribbean and Canada "

What if... THE USA HAD LAUNCHED AN INVASION OF CANADA?

military establishment was a growing body of opinion championed by imperialists who thought that the USA could and should be the world's only superpower. Coupled with this were the anti-British emotions stirred up by the jailing of Eamon de Valera, an American by birth who was arrested for his part in the 1916 Easter Rising. Throughout the 1920s, there were rearmament conferences in which the US imperialists metaphorically fought with the isolationists for control over hearts, minds and the military industrial complex. It became clear as the decade wore on that the imperialists were not going to gain a clear victory. So other more direct means would be needed. The first is what was called War Plan Red, this scheme for the USA to invade Canada and the Caribbean, and then destroy the Royal Navy, which in turn would destroy the British Empire. The second is a group of files called SPOBS, from the special observers group, based in and operating out of the American Embassy in London.

RIGHT
President Hoover and American delegates at the London Naval Conference in 1930

BELOW
An American tank on parade in Washington D.C.

This group in turn developed into the USAFBI which stood for United States of America Forces in the British Isles. With the eventual coming of American troops to the UK this was to become the European theatre of operation. So that sets the scene for basically what War Plan Red was, but also how it was linked to the later operations with huge amounts of spying activities operating out of the American Embassy in London. For example, they had well over 200 SPOBS members operating under the auspices of Ambassador Joseph Patrick Kennedy Senior in 1939.

Was the plan ever close to being initiated by America?
In terms of somebody pressing the button, 'We're gonna start War Plan Red', no, it never came close to that. From the documentation I've got you can see it was a continual process of revision with dated plans put forward annually. But it was all at a relatively low temperature. It was a cold war, ready for activation, but it never even got warm. And as the 1930s progressed, it became clear to the isolationists within the USA and the hawks within the War Department that there was little need for the Americans to force a regime change within the UK. 'We'll just let Hitler do it!' - that's how the impetus on War Plan Red slowly diminished. With the advent of the Nazis and Hitler in the mid 1930s there was no need for the Americans to risk financial involvement or American lives, whether we're talking invasion by sea using the navy, or an invasion on the ground using the army. They thought, 'We'll just let

> "If America destroyed the Royal Navy, the British Empire would be defenceless"

Hitler do it because Hitler's gonna knock the bridge'.

Did Britain have a similar plan?
I've looked as far as I can through our national archives, and I've looked through things like the *Hansard* parliamentary records, and I can't find anything. There doesn't appear to be anything comparable. The only thing that is remotely comparable are things like Churchill talking about strengthening the RAF, Army and Royal Navy, not necessarily to bring about regime change, but just to keep the British Empire going. But I haven't found anything in any way, shape or form of an equivalent for the British to get rid of other regimes.

If War Plan Red had gone ahead and war broken out with the British, what could have happened?
In my personal opinion, and I should stress this is only my view and not that of my publisher or editor, there are a few things that could have happened. There is a possibility that it could have succeeded but I don't think in terms of pure military strength the US at that time had the physical or financial means to do such a thing. When the American depression hit in 1929, they wouldn't have had the finance to do it. If you want to go 'what if?' to the extreme, it might well have been possible that America could have invaded the little islands in the Caribbean, which were part of the British Empire. What would have happened to Cuba? In the 1950s, Cuba and its dictator Batista were a good example of how the US had become financially involved in that sphere. If War Plan Red had ever happened, would Fidel Castro have evolved like he did with Russian influence? If Castro hadn't been in Cuba what about people like Che Guevara? That in turn affects what would have happened in South America. Don't forget that in the late 1940s and right throughout the 1950s and 1960s there was an awful lot of Soviet influence in South America. If America had invaded Canada? Well, that would have allowed America to link up with Alaska. Would the Canadians have gone along with it? I don't know but there was a lot of anti-British feeling among the French Canadians on the eastern seaboard.

How might 20th-century history have changed if War Plan Red had gone ahead?
We would almost certainly have had a different global aspect, but I don't think it would have stopped World War II. I don't think it would have stopped Hitler, and I don't think it would have stopped the Japanese. It just means that the red on the map would have gone a different colour or the red on the globe would have gone a different colour. But I still think there would have been all of the proxy wars in South America and Africa. It would have probably brought forth Stalin and the Soviets a bit sooner than they actually did.

All the colours of the rainbow

War Plan Red was one of a number of colour-coded plans created by the United States during the 1920s and 1930s. The plan that received the most attention was War Plan Orange, which focused on a war with Japan alone. War Plan Black dealt with a potential war with Germany and had several versions, one of which dealt with the possibility that France had been defeated at the end of World War I. The plan suggested possible ways to stop a German attempt to seize French territories in the Caribbean and stop an attack on the USA's eastern seaboard. There were also a number of multilateral plans that dealt with alliances (for example Red-Orange, which discussed the Anglo-Japanese alliance before its collapse in 1923). Following the start of conflict in Europe, the possibility of war on multiple fronts against a coalition of enemies led to the creation of the Rainbow plans, which combined and built upon the previous versions. When the United States entered WWII, some of War Plan Orange was used in its strategy against the Japanese.

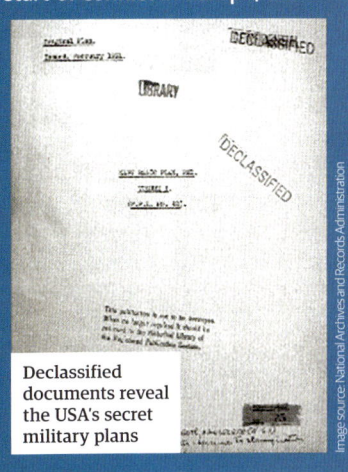

Declassified documents reveal the USA's secret military plans

What if...
NAPOLEON HAD WON AT TRAFALGAR?

Nelson's victory saved Britain from the threat of invasion, but could the British have lost the 1805 naval battle?

INTERVIEW WITH

Richard Harding
Professor Richard Harding is an expert in naval history and amphibious warfare and previously edited the academic journal, *The Mariner's Mirror*. Among his numerous books are *Modern Naval History: Debates and Prospects* and *Seapower and Naval Warfare: 1650-1830*.

RIGHT
John Christian Schetky's painting of the battle

On 21 October 1805, the naval forces of Napoleon Bonaparte and his Spanish allies faced the Royal Navy, commanded by Admiral Lord Nelson, off the coast of Trafalgar, Spain. For five hours the battle raged but the British forces were able to annihilate the enemy, destroying 19 ships. However, 1,500 British seamen lost their lives, with Nelson among them. Having been shot by a sniper in the shoulder and chest, he died when victory was imminent. The Battle of Trafalgar has become the stuff of legend, with Nelson immortalised as the man who saved Britain from invasion. Yet what if Napoleon had won on that fateful day?

What is some of the wider context leading up to Trafalgar?
Napoleon thought he would be able to trick the British and move them out of position, leaving the English Channel open. Napoleon's plan was to draw the British to the West Indies, then hopefully the French Commander Villeneuve would be able to go up the Channel and control a landing on the coast. That was never going to happen, though, because the British Channel fleet never moved. The British were well aware of this plan and everything they did was geared towards continuing to consolidate control of the Channel. I think Napoleon thought that he could threaten Britain with an invasion and pressure them into some kind of treaty. On the other side of the coin, Britain couldn't win the war with just its navy, though it could certainly defend itself. What Britain needed was allies, and they created an alliance with Russia, Sweden and Austria that would force Napoleon that way. The intention was to keep both the Baltic and the Mediterranean open, because Britain was earning vast sums of money from trade in those areas.

What were the key factors in the Battle of Trafalgar?
The battle was a very unequal struggle, despite the number of ships broadly being the same. When Napoleon finally got the Spanish to join with France, declaring war on Britain in October 1804, there were another 28 Spanish ships which could now support the 34 French ones. Another factor is Villeneuve himself. He was from an old family and of good standing, but by this point he was totally demoralised. He had survived the Battle of the Nile and knew what Nelson was capable of doing - Nelson's intention was annihilation. Napoleon was also losing faith in Villeneuve and he knew this. So what we've got in terms of key factors is a French fleet heading out to sea heading to the Mediterranean, with a commander that is thoroughly depressed. On the other side we've got a British fleet that knew exactly what it was doing at this point and was determined that this would be a battle of

What if…
NAPOLEON HAD WON AT TRAFALGAR?

What if... NAPOLEON HAD WON AT TRAFALGAR?

ABOVE An artist's impression of the scene aboard the French ship Algésiras during the battle

THE PAST

1789-99
THE RISE OF NAPOLEON
Napoleon Bonaparte had made his name as a young officer during the French Revolution. On 5 October 1795 he was instrumental in stopping Royalist rebels who were marching on the National Convention, saving the Republic. Appointed commander in chief of the army in Italy, he oversaw numerous victories and organised the Treaty of Campo Formio with Austria. In 1799 he organised a coup détat, seized control and proclaimed himself the emperor of France.

1777-98
WHO WAS HORATIO NELSON?
By the time he was commanding the British forces at Trafalgar, Nelson had already established himself as a top naval commander. In 1777 he had become a lieutenant and had fought in the American Revolutionary wars. After an unsuccessful stint commanding a frigate and enforcing the Navigation Act against American ships he was without another appointment for five years, when he then fought the Revolutionary French in the Mediterranean. His victory at the Battle of Cape St Vincent in 1797 won Nelson a knighthood and a promotion to rear admiral. Another victory, at the Battle of the Nile, saw Nelson all but annihilate the French forces.

1805-6
VILLENEUVE'S CAPTURE AND DEATH
Born into a noble and established family, Pierre-Charles Villeneuve received rapid promotion upon entering the French Navy. It was his flagship, along with one other, which were the only two to escape destruction at the hands of Nelson during the Battle of the Nile. Following defeat at Trafalgar, Villeneuve was captured but released shortly after, whereupon he returned to France in disgrace. Shortly after arriving and aware that Napoleon would be severely displeased with the defeat at Trafalgar, Villeneuve committed suicide. Stabbing himself six times in the chest, this caused some to speculate he'd in fact been murdered.

---

annihilation. The strongest navy was the combined fleet with about 33 ships, as opposed to the Royal Navy's 27, but the quality of the command and the quality of support was far different.

What were some of the immediate results of the battle?
It ended Napoleon's hopes of contesting the seas. It meant that he didn't have the capacity to be really disruptive in trying to attack the British colonies, either in the West Indies or in the East Indies. It didn't save Britain from the threat of invasion but it did ensure the security of British maritime communications and also secured British access to markets in the Mediterranean. Despite Napoleon's actions, most of Europe still wanted British goods. Due to their victory the British were able to import goods into Europe from the Mediterranean and the Baltic. However it did not have the dramatic impact of saving Britain from invasion, which I think is the crucial thing. The 19th and 20th century British narrative is that all that stood between Britain and the Napoleonic invasion was Nelson and a few ships, which simply wasn't the case.

Are there any instances where the combined fleet could have won?
Put simply, no. The French and Spanish performed a single line and Nelson had split his own line into two. Recently, during the Bicentenary, the battle was modelled on a computer and it was quite clear that what Nelson did as he approached the French and Spanish was to move as if he was going to attack further to the front of the French line. This caused Villeneuve to push his own line further out, so they couldn't support the two parts of the line which were cut. It was a pretty one-sided event. I can't see where during the battle that Villeneuve could have actually won.

What if the British government had not concluded the treaty of the Third Coalition with Austria in August 1805? Might that have meant Napoleon's Grand Armee was still on the Channel coast by the time a critical battle at sea occurred?
What strikes me about this whole affair was the importance of Britain negotiating the Third Coalition in getting Sweden and Russia on board, and by August involving Austria too. Once that happened Napoleon gave up any idea of invading Britain. He had to move his army to the east in order to confront the Austrians. If that hadn't happened, then the army would still have been on the Channel coast. Whether, despite that defeat, Napoleon would have tried to find other means is an interesting question. Again, though, highly difficult because you only have small ships to cross the channel in. He needed a long period of good weather and he needed to keep his communications open for probably six weeks. If the British hadn't concluded that treaty then it's possible that the

French might have found some kind of way to get across the Channel but it would have been a very small chance.

What if Villeneuve had been more aggressive in his approach to the Battle of Trafalgar?
This is a great point for French historians. Before Villeneuve was put in command there was an admiral called La Touche-Tréville and he had previously beaten Nelson. He was a different kettle of fish to Villeneuve, and he would also have stood up to Napoleon when he was making impossible demands. It's likely he would have also worked better with the Spanish as well, because the Spanish fleet was in relatively good condition and its officers were extremely good. Essentially you would have a far better naval commander, far stronger in terms of his relationships with his Spanish collaborators, and someone who would've stood up to Napoleon. That's one of the great questions surrounding the battle: what if someone who had fought Nelson and beaten him had been in command? The whole campaign would have been very different.

Could it have led to an invasion of England? Were there plans in place?
There was a whole series of plans, dating right back to revolutionary times, and Napoleon had a number of his own. But could a victory for him at Trafalgar have led to an invasion? It would have been extremely unlikely. Even if Britain had been defeated, the French and Spanish would've had to go on fighting their way up the Channel, defeating equally large forces with a reducing number of ships. I think I'm right in saying that Napoleon had estimated that he needed about 138,000 troops to capture London, and he only ever had the capacity to land 90,000. It's unlikely that one defeat of the British off the coast of southern Spain would have led to an invasion, but there were plans.

If Napoleon had won, what could some of the immediate consequences have been?
It would have put more pressure upon the British expedition to Southern Italy. Prior to the Battle of Trafalgar the British had sent a force to the Kingdom of Naples, with Russian support. As it happened, British attempts to stop the French invasion in Naples failed anyway, but it would have made it much more complicated.

Could a French victory at Trafalgar have had a wider historical impact?
If it had been a victory it would have put the seal on Napoleon's reputation as a strategic genius. If the Royal Navy had been thrown out of its position we would have a different view of Napoleon. In France, Napoleon's reputation as a land commander is almost second to none, but to me it was his ineptitude in many ways of understanding the sea that let him down. I think we would also have a different world in some respects because Britain would have become part of the Napoleonic empire, even if it were through giving up its colonial possessions. The British had taken numerous French colonies and it's likely that the French would have insisted that they took those back. So it was a big ask for a victory to take place, but it would have had a massive historical impact.

BELOW
The death of Nelson, who became immortalised as a British hero

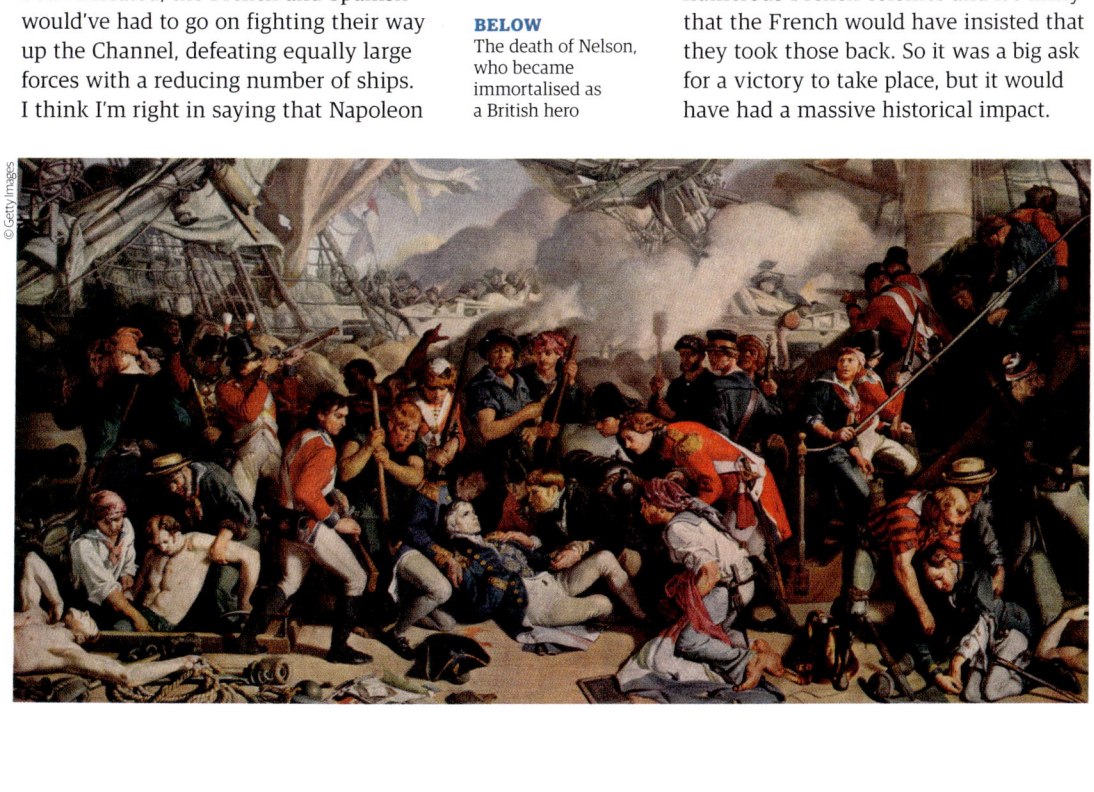

THE POSSIBILITY

1805
INVASION?
While Napoleon was in exile on St Helena towards the end of his life, he noted to his doctor, Barry O'Meara, that: "It was my firm intention to invade England and to head the expedition myself." Napoleon then outlined his plan of drawing off the Royal Navy, then sail up the Channel and land an army that would march on and seize the capital. O'Meara described how the two became involved in a debate as to the viability of such a plan and whether the British population would not have resisted and taken to the streets to defend the city. However, interestingly, Napoleon claimed that during the proposed march on London he would have exercised the most extreme discipline towards his troops and that he would have come to Britain as a 'friend' of the people. He said: "Marauding or otherwise injuring or insulting the inhabitants would have been punished with instant death."

1803
LA TOUCHE-TRÉVILLE
In 1803, Admiral Louis-René de La Touche-Tréville had successfully managed to hold back the forces of Nelson while at Boulogne. In 1804, while off Toulon, La Touche-Tréville intercepted Nelson as he was on the way to capture two French vessels. Nelson turned back, followed by La Touche-Tréville, who then used the event to publicly humiliate the British admiral. For Nelson's part, this began a bitter rivalry and he insulted his adversary numerous times. For La Touche-Tréville, he spoke of a desire to "have another confrontation with his colleague, Nelson". La Touche-Tréville died in 1804 but had he lived to see Trafalgar it may have been he, and not Villeneuve, who commanded the French/Spanish forces. If so, it would have been the final titanic duel between two rivals.

What if...

ARGENTINA HAD WON THE FALKLANDS WAR?

Margaret Thatcher gambled on direct military action. But an Argentine victory could have left both her and Britain's reputation in tatters

INTERVIEW WITH

Professor Richard Toye
Richard is professor of Modern History at the University of Exeter. He has published more than 20 books, including *Age of Hope: Labour, 1945, and the Birth of Modern Britain* (Bloomsbury Continuum, 2023).

Following the Argentinian incursion into the Falklands, the move by Margaret Thatcher to deploy a military task force to retake the territory galvanised a nation. Britain seemed to be united in a patriotic fervour and single-minded belief that it had been deeply wronged and was taking action to show it was still a major player to be reckoned with on the world stage. Following the British victory, and a hero's welcome for the task force, Thatcher would refer to the 'Falklands Spirit' for years to come. But with a British failure in the South Atlantic, the global respect afforded Margaret Thatcher might never have materialised, and there could have been serious repercussions for Britain, at home and around the world.

What may have been the impact on global politics and Britain's reputation if Britain had lost?
This depends on the exact scenario. One possibility would have been that the UK's political and military leadership decided that action to recapture the islands was simply too risky, and that it should just be accepted. Another is that military action was tried but failed – possible if the Americans had not given critical intelligence and logistical help. The first outcome would have been easier to survive than the second. Few people in Britain even knew where the Falklands were, and though the issue could not exactly have been brushed under the carpet, it would have been possible to try to manage it diplomatically, and through economic sanctions. This was what had been tried after Rhodesia's Unilateral Declaration of Independence (UDI) in 1965, and although the Rhodesian question became a running sore in British politics, it never brought down a government. Once a task force had sailed to the South Atlantic, though, the stakes were much higher. Defeat would have been reminiscent of the 1956 Suez Crisis (albeit that was a diplomatic catastrophe surrounding a successful military operation). In terms of global reputation, it would likely have confirmed impressions of Britain as a declining power with failed imperial pretensions. Certainly, it would have been harder for Thatcher (or any replacement prime minister) to present herself as a serious player on the world stage. Although Britain's impact on the end of the Cold War should not be overstated, Thatcher deserves credit for recognising Mikhail Gorbachev as a Soviet leader with whom it was possible to do business. She was also widely admired in Eastern Europe. It is hard to envisage things turning out quite the same way if Britain had recently experienced military humiliation, though.

What boost would a win have given the military dictatorship in Argentina and how would that impact on the country's future?
Victory would doubtless have given the Argentine Junta a significant boost, but equally clearly it would not have solved the fundamental political, economic,

RIGHT
Falklands sovereignty has been disputed for more than a century

What if...
ARGENTINA HAD WON THE FALKLANDS WAR?

What if... ARGENTINA HAD WON THE FALKLANDS WAR?

THE PAST

PRE-1982

CLAIM AND COUNTERCLAIM

The issue of sovereignty over the Falklands Islands had been a matter of dispute between Britain and Argentina since the early 19th century. By 1833, Great Britain had established the islands, basically using gunboat diplomacy, as British territory. For more than a century the dispute rumbled on in the background, an ever-present agenda item for British-Argentine diplomatic relations. In 1982, under the military Junta led by Leopoldo Galtieri, the voices grew much louder. Things were not going well at home for the generals, with eye-watering inflation and human rights abuses against their opponents. They needed a glorious victory to reunite the country, and their attention turned to the Falkland Islands.

MAR – APR 1982

THE OTHER SIDE OF THE WORLD

On 19 March 1982, a group of salvage workers raised the Argentine flag on the island of South Georgia, also British Territory. On 2 April, Argentina invaded the Falklands and later that month had 10,000 troops on the islands. Thatcher's government declared a war exclusion zone around the islands. On 5 April, a British task force led by two aircraft carriers set sail for the South Atlantic. By 25 April, South Georgia was recaptured. The sinking of the Argentine cruiser, General Belgrano, by a British nuclear submarine kept most of the Argentine fleet in port.

1982-83

VICTORY AWAY GIVES VICTORY AT HOME

There were considerable losses of aircraft and ships on both sides, but Argentina could never create the dominance in the air to stop a land invasion. Following an amphibious landing, British troops started their assault. They faced a fierce and determined defence, but on 14 June, the Argentine forces surrendered. Success in the South Atlantic meant a hero's welcome on the return of the Task Force. It also assured victory for Thatcher and the Conservatives in the 1983 election. The reputations of both Britain and its prime minister were intact.

and social problems from which the invasion was designed to distract. On 6 April 1982, around a quarter of a million people gathered before the presidential palace in Buenos Aires in support of the Falklands/Malvinas invasion. Yet they also voiced their opposition to the Junta. The opposition was determined to demand sweeping change once the war was over – whether it was won or lost. Triumph on the battlefield would have given the regime breathing space – but it would not have forestalled its probably inevitable collapse.

In short, a different outcome to the war would not have averted the Argentinian political instability that persists to this day. It is also interesting to ask, though, if the USA could have maintained better relations with Latin America had it not decided to back Britain – a move seen widely across the region as a betrayal.

What would a loss have meant for Margaret Thatcher and for the Conservative Party?

Whereas acceptance of the situation might have been politically survivable, that was not Thatcher's style. Once she had committed herself to taking back the islands by force, her future prospects were inevitably tied to the operation's success. If it had failed unambiguously, she would have had to resign. The question is, who would have taken over? There were a number of able ministers in the Cabinet. Three of them, Willie Whitelaw, Jim Prior, and Geoffrey Howe, had been defeated by Thatcher for the leadership in 1975. Of these, Howe, as chancellor of the exchequer, might have been the most plausible contender, but there could also have been wildcards such as the ambitious environment secretary, Michael Heseltine.

What, though, would have been the outcome for the ideological direction of the Conservatives? In 1982, Thatcher was in the process of converting the party to her brand of economics, but still had to be mindful of the divisions between 'wets' and 'dries'. Howe was fully signed up to the free market agenda but might have lacked the force of personality to drive through radical change by himself. Defeat in the Falklands would certainly have strengthened the hand of those who had long been sceptical of Thatcher's approach, even though her economic policies would not obviously have been discredited by military failure as such. In other words, Tory divisions would have been exacerbated,

ABOVE-LEFT
Margaret Thatcher staked her reputation on the Task Force

ABOVE-RIGHT
General Galtieri hoped victory would settle unrest at home

BELOW
Captured Argentinian soldiers were repatriated

and if Thatcher had remained on the backbenches, she would have had little incentive to hold her tongue.

What public opinion issues would need to be managed in Britain?

The despatch of the Task Force was accompanied by an upsurge in jingoistic feeling. Defeat in the South Atlantic would surely have led to a sense of crushing disappointment, even betrayal, likely much encouraged by parts of the popular press. This was also a time of mass unemployment and considerable industrial strife. The loss of the war could have had repercussions for Britain's global economic standing,

which would have made these problems even harder to manage. However, Suez offered a precedent for the Conservatives in how to successfully deal with a heavy reputational blow. Anthony Eden quickly stood down on grounds of ill health and his successor, Harold Macmillan, moved quickly to mend relations with the USA, while maintaining a world statesperson image which seemed to suggest that nothing very damaging had happened. Although it is difficult to see exactly how the same trick could have been pulled off in the conditions of the 1980s, the Conservatives have historically been very good at sustaining themselves in power even in spite of major crises and obvious failures. However, the loss of the Falklands would certainly have dented their reputation as the patriotic party, and a new threat might have emerged from the right.

Would a loss have meant Labour won the 1983 election?
This seems far from certain. The Labour Party was extremely divided and its leader, Michael Foot, was not widely regarded as a credible prime minister. If the Conservatives had ditched Thatcher and adopted a more consensual style of politics, they might actually have increased their appeal. That said, the Tories would have faced an enormous challenge, and the prospect of election victory might have led Labour to act in a more united way. It could conceivably have squeaked a narrow majority.

> "The Tories would have faced an enormous challenge, and the prospect of election victory might have led Labour to act in a more united way"

However, there is another possibility. The Social Democratic Party (SDP) broke away from the Labour Party in 1981. Prior to the Falklands, it rode high in the polls, and in fact (in alliance with the Liberals) scored a quarter of the votes in the 1983 election. If the Conservatives had been discredited by defeat, and if Labour had failed to solve its internal and policy issues, the SDP-Liberal Alliance could have been significantly strengthened. The first-past-the-post electoral system tends to favour the two main parties. This makes it unlikely that the Alliance would have been able to form a government in its own right unless its performance was truly spectacular. However, if the Conservatives, Labour, and the Alliance had all secured 33 per cent shares, the Alliance could have emerged as a potential kingmaker/coalition partner. Perhaps a Geoffrey Howe-Roy Jenkins partnership would have rendered the Cameron-Clegg coalition historically unnecessary.

How would domestic and economic politics in the UK have looked in the years after a defeat, and since?
Let us continue with the Tory-Alliance coalition scenario. The Conservatives moderate their policies, undertaking only a few further modest privatisations and tax cuts, and making common cause with their Alliance partners in favour of European integration. At a further election in 1987, the Alliance emerges as the largest party and Jenkins becomes prime minister. When he retires through ill health, David Owen, foreign secretary, enters No 10. When the Berlin Wall falls he gains a temporary boost from the 'peace dividend'. But his personality is too abrasive to maintain unity, and though he squeezes out a narrow surprise victory in 1992, the British people are tired with the politics of the centre ground and are instead looking for a new approach. The Labour Party revives and in 1997 wins a landslide victory under an MP from the 1983 intake with radical left-wing credentials. His name is Tony Blair.

THE POSSIBILITY

1983

THE IRON LADY MELTS
It is unlikely, having staked so much of her reputation – and that of her party – on the defence of the Falkland Islands, that Margaret Thatcher would have been able to politically survive an Argentine victory. With loss of face, and faith, in the eyes of the electorate she would have become a liability for the Conservatives. At worst it would mean outright defeat in the polls. At best, some form of coalition with the rising SDP party could be struck. But without Thatcher as leader, or perhaps even the Tories in opposition, pivotal moments in history, such as the Brighton Bombing by the IRA, may never have come to pass.

1981 ONWARDS

NEW KIDS ON THE BLOCK
Although the newly formed Social Democratic Party (SDP) was rising in popularity, it probably wouldn't have been able to form a government on its own. That's not to say it would not wield power. In alliance with the Liberal Party, it had shown it could attract votes. With a weak Labour leadership and a fractured Tory party, such an alliance could have squeezed enough votes to govern. If not, then a more traditional pact with either Conservatives or Labour as the power behind the throne, would have meant 'Thatcherism' lost its focus and its relevance.

1984

SOFT LINE NOT PICKET LINE
With British social and economic policy taking a more restrained route, a number of things may have been different. Through the influence of more moderate voices – either from within the Tories or from coalition partners – the push for privatisations of public utilities may never have got off the ground. And industrial relations may possibly have been far more conciliatory. In 1984, the threat to the coal industry through pit closures dominated the news, and the political agenda. Government and unions were locked in a war of attrition, and running battles on the picket lines have become a symbol of British politics of the day. But with a victory for Argentina in the Falklands, this time could all have been so different.

What if...

OPERATION VALKYRIE HAD ASSASSINATED HITLER?

If desperate members of Hitler's closest circle seized one last chance to eliminate the Nazi leader, would the course of history be forever changed?

INTERVIEW WITH

Roger Moorhouse

Moorhouse is an award-winning historian and author of the critically acclaimed *Killing Hitler: The Third Reich and the Plots against the Führer*.

By July 1944 the Allied armies were back on European soil. As they began to push east towards Germany, the Nazi conspirators of Operation Valkyrie triggered their plan to blow up Adolf Hitler. The reclusive and paranoid dictator was encircled by a ring of steel and secrecy within his Wolf's Lair complex in Eastern Prussia, which only the most trusted could penetrate. Numerous attempts to kill him had failed, but on 20 July 1944 it was within his own stronghold that a bomb in a briefcase came tantalisingly close to wiping out perhaps the most notorious dictator of the 20th century and changing the course of World War II.

What made the conspirators of Operation Valkyrie believe they could succeed where previous attempts had failed?
I don't think the Valkyrie conspirators were necessarily more confident that they would succeed. As much as anything, theirs was a desperate act. It was a throw of the dice and a symbolic gesture - as one of their number said at the time - "to show that another Germany existed." What set them apart from the previous plots and attempts on Hitler's life was that they realised that it was no longer enough simply to assassinate their target. To achieve just this would leave a whole range of uncertainties and far too much to chance. They had to launch a coup to seize power as well. This made their task infinitely more complex and heightened the possibility of failure.

Of course, the great advantage that the Valkyrie conspirators had was that they had access to Hitler. By 1944, the German leader was a virtual recluse who was barely seen in public and had a highly refined and effective personal security regime. Anyone trying to target him would have to get through numerous levels of layered security checks, but a senior military officer coming to a briefing could avoid all that. What they were unable to plan for was the intervention of sheer chance. The briefcase containing the bomb was moved from its spot right next to Hitler, where it would've almost guaranteed his death, when Colonel Heinz Brandt inadvertently pushed it further under the table. He was just making room for himself, but in so doing the thick oak table leg shielded Hitler from the explosion. He escaped with just shredded trousers and a perforated eardrum. Those who'd plotted the bombing and attempted coup would eventually not be so fortunate.

Was there enough popular support, military strength and leadership to pull off a coup after Hitler's death? Would it have replaced bad with bad?
The civilian side of the plot was reasonably numerous and wide-ranging, but it is highly dubious that they could have taken power on 20 July, let alone held on to it. For one thing, the extent of popular

RIGHT
This reconstruction shows Hitler's position and that of the briefcase containing the bomb

What if...
OPERATION VALKYRIE HAD ASSASSINATED HITLER?

What if... OPERATION VALKYRIE HAD ASSASSINATED HITLER?

THE PAST

1939
IF AT FIRST YOU DON'T SUCCEED...

Assassination attempts on the German dictator were nothing new and there had been numerous other failed plots to dispose of him, such as in 1939 in a beer hall in Munich. A timebomb was planted, and the explosion killed others but not Hitler because he had already left the event. Other attempts over years, and their subsequent failures, only served to increase an eerie sense of invincibility, both in Hitler's own eyes and in those of the millions who looked to him for leadership, inspiration and strength.

JUNE 1944
ALLIES BACK IN EUROPE

With Operation Overlord on 6 June 1944 – D-Day – the tide of the war changed dramatically in favour of the Allies. It became increasingly clear that it was not a case of 'if' the Germans would lose the war, but 'when'. Becoming ever more withdrawn within a much-reduced inner circle of only his most trusted military advisors, a deluded Hitler continued to plan his strategy to repel the advancing Allies. But for many high-ranking German soldiers and officials, waiting for the Allies to rid them of Hitler was unthinkable – they had to grasp the moment for themselves.

JULY 1944
A PLAN IN TATTERS

Being so close to the Führer was all in a day's work for Colonel Claus Schenk Graf von Stauffenberg. That was the easy part. But for all the planning it was to be a stroke of fate that left the plot in ruins when the briefcase bomb under the table was moved at the last moment. As he fled the scene von Stauffenberg made the fatal error of assuming Hitler was dead. Mixed messages flew around the airwaves, but it was not so. They had failed. Hitler had survived with only minor injuries and torn trousers. His retribution was swift, with the conspirators and thousands of other suspects rounded up and executed.

---

support [for an assassination and coup] is rather questionable. Of course, there were many ordinary Germans who were tired of the war by July 1944, and some of them might have felt freed from their loyalty to the regime by the death of Hitler, but such was the power of Nazi propaganda and control that I doubt it would have been enough to sustain the coup.

In addition, the coup plotters lacked the determination and grit to do what was necessary. Instead of executing their senior opponents, it seems they preferred to effectively inherit power by assassination. Anyone of senior rank in the public eye who was not eliminated would only be a rallying point for further unrest and resistance to change. So in reality their actions did not match the enormity of the task in hand. They had recognised the need to not only assassinate Hitler but also launch a coup to take control, but perhaps naively they convinced themselves that the demise of Hitler would somehow trigger a popular response that would take on its own momentum to meet their objectives. Had they been more brutal they might have had a better chance of success.

Is it possible there would have been a civil war in Germany?
Civil war was always a possibility, but it would have required some sort of popular uprising against Nazi rule. In order to achieve this, the plotters would've had to overcome some overwhelming challenges: the sheer weight of the years that the Nazi regime had been in power, the charismatic hold of Hitler himself that was still at the centre of the message (even though by this time he was rarely seen in public), and the reach and depth of the Nazi information and propaganda machine. And it could have led to a more fractured country with various and complex factions looking for an opportunity to gain from the unrest and uncertainty. As it was, the Valkyrie plotters needed to dupe most of the army units operating in their name into believing that they were acting in support of the Nazi regime, but that ruse would not have worked for more than a few hours. For any sort of prolonged confrontation to be won, the plotters would have needed a large slice of popular support.

Under what terms would the new leadership have surrendered to the Allies? Or would they have fought on, and with what possible outcome?
Had they managed to secure control of the levers of power, the coup plotters wanted to agree terms with the Western

TOP-INSET
Field Marshal Errwin von Witzleben was executed along with other high-ranking conspirators

ABOVE
Nazi officials examine the aftermath of the explosion. Four people were killed but Hitler survived

LEFT
Claus Schenk Graf von Stauffenberg was close to Adolf Hitler and planted the bomb

and Russia? How would the map of Europe have been affected? And what about Italy?

It is tempting to imagine that a seizure of power by the coup plotters in July 1944 could have caused profound change to the circumstances that we know played out. However, any significant change would have been dependent on the new German regime being able to persuade the Western Powers to effectively abandon their Soviet ally and sign up to a separate peace. It would also have relied heavily on how the new leaders of Germany were dealing with any possible domestic unrest caused by the coup. How would any unrest impact their ability to be effective partners, politically and militarily, in a rapidly conceived alliance against the Soviets? The Allies would also have to be convinced that the new leadership stood as one, with a single vision and determination which went beyond just a Germany without Hitler, or even Nazis. The idea of substantial change to the geo-political landscape post-coup, therefore, is a chimera, an unrealistic vision. The constellation of power ranged against Germany by 1944 was too great to effectively dismantle.

What would the impact on the war in the Far East have been and why?
There is a possibility that the war in the Far East might have seen some impact. Obviously the Allied forces were fighting on a separate front in a completely different part of the world, and with that came enormous logistical and tactical issues which extra forces could have helped to alleviate even a little. With a separate peace in Europe, it would theoretically have been possible for the United States to transfer more of its forces to the Pacific theatre, thereby bringing more pressure to bear on the Japanese. This in turn may have had some impact on how and when the Allies would and could have defeated Japan. Given enough time and resources it may have considered a full invasion of the Japanese mainland itself. One might speculate that a swifter Japanese collapse could have meant that deployment of the atomic bomb could have been avoided, and as such the actual use of such a weapon in combat would have remained very much on the drawing board as a theoretical and untried tactic.

However, given that any transfer of American troops would have likely taken months to put into effect, one must wonder whether the effect of such a shift might actually have been minimal.

Powers while fighting on against the Soviets. But for any of that to be feasible, any terms had to be realistic, achievable and not imbalanced in such a way that Germany was merely just trying to soften the blow of defeat. It was from the East that the Germans feared for their future more than anything, from a Soviet Union that would inflict its revenge for what it had suffered at the hands of Nazi Germany. This was perhaps an understandable ambition from a German conservative perspective, but it flew in the face of the many expressions of Allied unity – not least the Casablanca Declaration of 1943, which demanded the unconditional surrender of Axis forces. In such circumstances, I think it's doubtful that any separate peace with the Allies would have been possible.

As the plot was before the 1945 Yalta Conference, how could its success have changed the Western Allies' ambitions in relation to Germany

THE POSSIBILITY

1944

FROM FOE TO FRIEND
Had the plot succeeded, it's possible (however remote) that the Germans may have surrendered and struck a deal with the Western Allies. From bitter experience the Germans knew just what kind of adversary the Russians could be, and they knew the terrible suffering inflicted by the Nazis would never be forgiven. If the Germans could somehow play on any doubts the West had about their Russian partners – and what they intended to gain from the war – then the Western Allies might, just might, be tempted to ally with Germany to keep the Russians out of Europe...

1945 – PRESENT

NOT-SO-COLD WAR
If the West had helped Germany escape the clutches of the Russian advance, perhaps persuaded by the inevitable division of territories and natural resources held by the Nazis around the world, then the present-day map of Europe may have looked very different. The possibilities seem endless: no Warsaw Pact countries, no Iron Curtain, no divided Germany and no Berlin Wall. The influence of the Soviet Union would be substantially diminished in the post-war era and the rising star of the United States would shine even more brightly.

1945

A DIFFERENT KIND OF SURRENDER
If the conflict in Europe had ended more quickly there could have been a dramatic impact on the war against Japan. In time, more troops, ships and armour could have been redeployed to the Far East to the point which, perhaps, an invasion of Japan itself would've been a distinct possibility. There would have been a much higher cost to pay in casualties on both sides, but if Japan had been overwhelmed by conventional forces then maybe the use of the atom bomb wouldn't have been necessary to bring about its surrender.

What if...
THE USA HAD WON THE VIETNAM WAR?

With the US successful in Vietnam, it could have adopted a more aggressive, less gun-shy foreign policy...

INTERVIEW WITH

Dr Andrew Wiest

Dr Andrew Wiest lectures at the University of Southern Mississippi. His books include *The Boys Of '67: Charlie Company's War In Vietnam*, *Vietnam's Forgotten Army: Heroism And Betrayal In The ARVN* and *Vietnam: A View From The Front Lines*. He has also organised trips for Vietnam veterans suffering from PTSD to visit the country they once fought in.

RIGHT
A man suspected of supporting the Viet Cong forces being arrested and detained by US forces

FAR RIGHT
If the US campaign in Vietnam had proven successful, we might have seen an even greater influx of American influence than has already happened

What would have happened if the United States had won the Vietnam War?

There are a lot of academics and historians who look at Vietnam as a part of something much bigger – namely, the Cold War. So if the United States had won, the Cold War would probably have ended a little sooner, and the dawn of that unilateral superpower controlling things would have come quicker. In Southeast Asia, everything would be radically different – including a faster and more thorough confrontation between the US and China. I doubt China would have sat by and let an American victory happen without repercussion – even though they were not exactly fans of the Vietnamese either. I don't think Beijing would have invaded Vietnam to repel the Americans, as they did in Korea, but it certainly would have been the US against China and Russia. And it would have been a war that was not just cold but glacial. American politics would certainly have been more tumultuous as well.

If you look at the US presidential elections since the 1960s, every one of them has been fought over Vietnam to one extent or another. It is still the most controversial aspect of a controversial time period. Had they come out of that smiling, with another greatest generation on their hands, politics in the US would have looked quite different. For instance, it is hard to see the Republican revolution taking place. Republicans typically have an aggressive foreign policy – it is one of their tropes – but if Democratic policy had won in Vietnam – because it was the Democrats who started the war in Southeast Asia – that would have taken a lot of heat away from their rivals.

Would the US have become involved in more conflicts?

Yes, I think the US would have been much less gun-shy during the 1970s and 1980s. Reagan tinkered with it, but that use of force to solve conflicts didn't really come back until the first Bush and then with Bill Clinton. The reason the US did not rely on its military, on any great scale at least, to solve problems during the 1970s and the 1980s was all down to the country's failure in Vietnam.

When the Vietnam War began to cross into Cambodia, it created the environment in which Pol Pot and the Khmer Rouge came to power. What resulted was a four-year holocaust. Could this have been avoided?

If the US was ever going to win the Vietnam War, it would have been during the Tet Offensive of 1968. That was the turning point, and that was when the public, back in the United States, saw the North Vietnamese were not just going to retreat and surrender – it was literally a fight to the death. Of course, there was no big, magical American victory during Tet, but let's imagine there was. Let's imagine the US had repelled that attack quickly and conclusively, and the war was essentially over as a result. At that point in time, the Khmer Rouge was not a big player in the conflict. It is only after the US began its military incursions into Cambodia, and the government in that country began to fall, that everything became out of hand. A victorious US in Vietnam would not have required any entrance into Cambodia, and as a result, you almost certainly would not have seen the rise of the Khmer Rouge. They are intrinsically tied to how the Vietnam War progressed, no doubt about that.

What if... THE USA HAD WON THE VIETNAM WAR?

A SUCCESSFUL CAMPAIGN

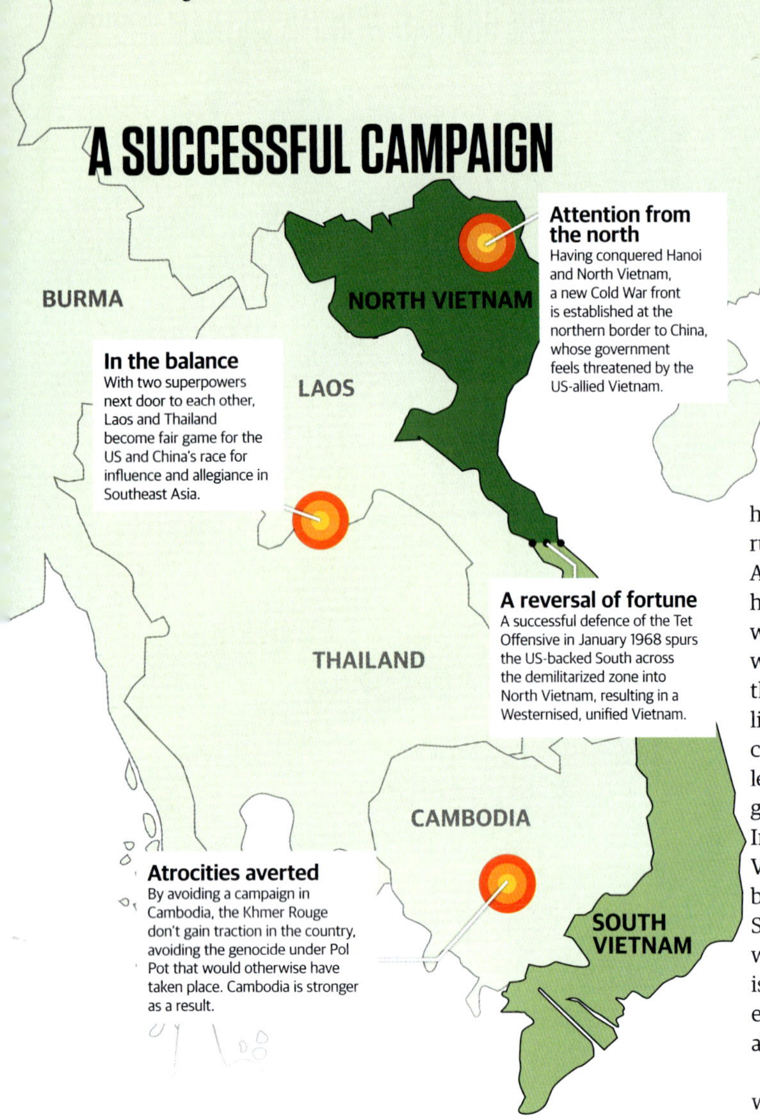

Attention from the north
Having conquered Hanoi and North Vietnam, a new Cold War front is established at the northern border to China, whose government feels threatened by the US-allied Vietnam.

In the balance
With two superpowers next door to each other, Laos and Thailand become fair game for the US and China's race for influence and allegiance in Southeast Asia.

A reversal of fortune
A successful defence of the Tet Offensive in January 1968 spurs the US-backed South across the demilitarized zone into North Vietnam, resulting in a Westernised, unified Vietnam.

Atrocities averted
By avoiding a campaign in Cambodia, the Khmer Rouge don't gain traction in the country, avoiding the genocide under Pol Pot that would otherwise have taken place. Cambodia is stronger as a result.

Would we ever have seen a situation like in Korea where the communist North and the democratic South are split down the middle, even to this day?

No, that was never going to happen. One side was going to reunify the country, no matter what. So, if there was a big American victory, one situation you have is reunification under non-communist rule. As a result of that, the turn towards Asia the US is presently taking would have happened then as opposed to now. We would have had an immediate conflict with China. Unlike the North Koreans, the North Vietnamese were much less likely to accept the scenario where the country remained split. If you look at their leadership - at their proclamations and their goals - they were not going to go for a 'tie'. In addition, the tactical situation in Vietnam was much trickier. This is because the border between North and South Vietnam is so long and porous that it would be very difficult to police - and that is why you had the Ho Chi Minh trail, the excursions into Cambodia and Laos and all of that other stuff.

So, it might be convenient to think that we could replay the Korean War and end Vietnam with a stalemate, but that was never going to happen. People forget they wanted reunification, too - just under different circumstances.

If John F. Kennedy had not been assassinated, would the Vietnam War have been avoided?

That is a controversial question. There have been so many arguments about this - and, of course, Kennedy's legacy is such a sacred thing in the States that it is political kryptonite to touch it. The pro-Kennedy forces argue he wanted to withdraw most of the 16,000 military advisors that were over there. However, before Kennedy, there were only 600 military advisors over there. He had begun a war over there, and I think there are two things that still would have hamstrung him even if he had wanted out. The first is that he still wanted his political party to win another term, and if the Democrats had wiped their hands of Vietnam, there is a good chance they would not have achieved that. The second is that Kennedy wanted his brother to be the next man in the White House. To mess that up - by handing Vietnam to the communists - would have sunk this. I would also argue that Robert McNamara, who was Kennedy's confidant in the first place and the architect of the Vietnam War, was going to give him the same advice he gave Lyndon B Johnson - which was to go in with all guns blazing. You have to remember that both Kennedy and Johnson faced the post-World War II consensus: to fight a difficult, problematic and long war against what they perceived as a communist threat or to

> "If the US was ever going to win the Vietnam War it would have been during the Tet Offensive of 1968"

HOW WOULD IT BE DIFFERENT?

REAL TIMELINE

1945

Vietnamese Declaration of Independence
Based on the American Declaration of Independence, Ho Chi Minh asks the US and the West to oppose French colonial rule in Vietnam and support what will be "a free and independent country".
2 September 1945

Ho Chi Minh contacts President Truman
The Vietnamese revolutionary writes to Truman asking him to "urgently interfere" in the foreign rule of his country. Truman fears Vietnam becoming communist and instead backs the French.
28 February 1946

ALTERNATE TIMELINE

The Geneva Conference
France agrees to the decolonisation of Vietnam. Free elections are promised, but the US suspects the communist Ho Chi Minh may win. It installs a brutal dictator, Ngo Dinh Diem, in South Vietnam. He is viewed by Ho Chi Minh and the North as a puppet ruler.
21 July 1954

Assassination of Đình Diêm
Diem – whose anti-Buddhist policies famously caused the monk Thich Quang Duc to immolate himself – is murdered in a brutal but mysterious coup d'état.
2 November 1963

US reunites Korea
Fears that China would support the North prove unfounded. The US manages to push back the comparatively minimal army of Kim Il-sung and successfully reunites the two Koreas. Seoul aligns itself as a Western-friendly government.
27 July 1953

ABOVE
A convoy of US tanks in Vietnam

embark on social changes back home - in particular, the civil rights movement. I think Kennedy was going to veer toward the civil rights movement - just as Johnson did. But I don't think you get both - civil rights and the end of Vietnam. That mixture would have brought the Democrats down at the voting booth.

Is there any way the Vietnam War may have been avoided?
Asking anyone to do the right thing back then was difficult. Had Franklin Roosevelt lived, maybe things could have been avoided. He had a guy on his team who was a communist, namely Stalin, and Roosevelt was not a fan of European colonialism. So he may have sided with Ho Chi Minh's desire to have an independent Vietnam, free from French rule. Had he lived longer, with all of his clout, I think that is the best chance we would have had to avoid starting a war.

Vietnam is now engulfed with examples of American culture. So who really won the war?
WeWell, that is the thing - they are now US allies. It shows, as Sun Tzu said, the best tool to win a war is not always the military. It was American culture that eventually prevailed.

If you look at things like Rambo and all these other Hollywood movies that attempted to justify the conflict, it is obvious how much impact it had on the United States. But it was just a blip on the radar to the Vietnamese. It cost them many more lives, but it was all part of a bigger struggle for independence.

Today, Vietnam has a huge young generation, and this is all ancient history to them. They have moved on, but ironically, it is the face of the US they now buy into.

- **Gulf of Tomkin fabrication**
North Vietnamese ships are reported to have fired on a US patroller, the Maddox, in the South China Sea. President Johnson uses the event to justify going to war. Declassified documents later confirmed that no attack happened. **2 August 1964**

- **The My Lai Massacre**
At My Lai, families are raped, tortured and killed by US soldiers. Lieutenant William Calley, who instigated the horror, walks free, but world opinion becomes opposed to 'America's war'. **16 March 1968**

- **Paris Peace Accords**
Nixon's government agrees to a ceasefire, with US ground troops and POWs returning home. The reunification of Vietnam is now a matter between the respective Saigon and Hanoi governments. **27 January 1973**

- **Fall of Saigon**
The war ends with the North Vietnamese taking Saigon by force and celebrating a reunified country. Ho Chi Minh, who died in 1969, remains a national icon. Saigon is now known as Ho Chi Minh City. **30 April 1975**

- **Tet Offensive**
On Vietnamese New Year, the North surprises the South with a sudden offensive. The city of Hue witnesses extensive fighting. South Vietnam and its allies suffer drastic losses. **30 January - 3 March 1968**

- **Ho Chi Minh at the UN**
Ho Chi Minh gives a rousing speech at the UN, but with the new Korea becoming an international trading partner, western nations side with the US on Vietnamese reunification. **December 1956**

- **Gulf of Tomkin fabrication**
Johnson, respecting Kennedy's opposition to communism in Asia and Latin America, fabricates the Gulf of Tonkin incident to justify entering the war in Vietnam. **2 August 1964**

- **Failed Tet Offensive**
The North Vietnamese conduct a failed attempt to take Saigon, Hue and other cities in South Vietnam. Forewarned about the attack, the US Army repels their enemies. **30 January - 14 February 1968**

- **Free elections**
Pressured into elections, US fears come true and Ho Chi Minh becomes president of Vietnam. However, believing this would expose the South Vietnamese to communist rule, the Eisenhower government argues the elections were fixed. **January 1956**

- **Fixed elections?**
Eisenhower releases a statement claiming that, "After an extensive CIA investigation we can reveal the elections in Vietnam were rigged." South Vietnam is to continue with a 'democratic' regime headed by an interim coalition of allied countries. **March 1956**

- **Kennedy's speech**
Concluding with how close the world came to nuclear war during the Cuban Missile Crisis, President Kennedy affirms that all communist countries must be treated as rogue states. Military involvement is increased heavily in Vietnam. **October 1962**

- **Cambodia's involvement**
The White House offers to supply Cambodia's Communist Party of Kampuchea guerrilla fighters in aid and arms if they can offer the US details of the Ho Chi Minh trail supply route. The deal is only revealed decades later. **August 1967**

- **Fall of Hanoi**
On Ho Chi Minh's birthday, the North Vietnam capital collapses under the military might of the US army. The war is over. China becomes so concerned that Mao immediately agrees to a trade pact with Coca-Cola. **19 May 1968**

What if...

THE USSR HAD INVENTED THE ATOMIC BOMB FIRST?

A Soviet victory in the race for the atomic bomb could have meant a very different Cold War

INTERVIEW WITH

David J Holloway

David J Holloway is professor emeritus at Stanford University and the author of *Stalin and the Bomb: The Soviet Union and Atomic Energy, 1939-1956* (1994) and the essay *Nuclear Weapons and the Cold War in Europe* (2013).

RIGHT
Mushroom cloud over Nagasaki

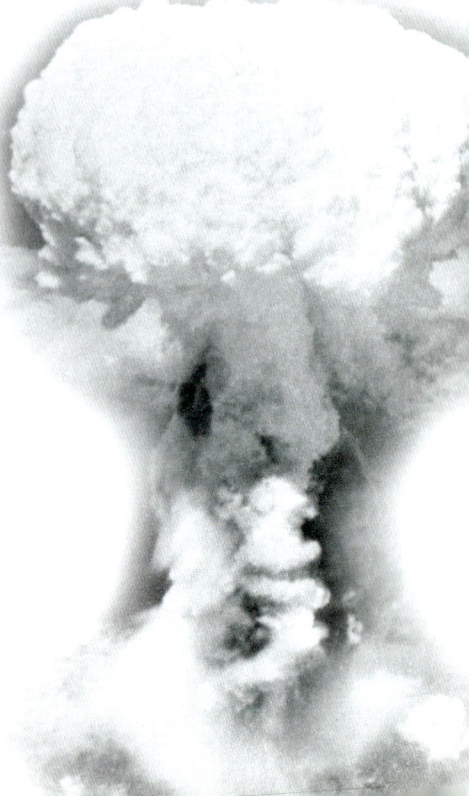

When physicists Lise Meitner and Otto Frisch discovered nuclear fission in December 1938, the possibility of an atomic weapon became a frightening reality. Scientists from several countries began work, seeking to produce such a device. However, after being invaded by Nazi Germany in 1941, the Soviet Union chose instead to focus efforts on repelling the enemy. Meanwhile, in the United States, the Manhattan Project saw a team of experts led by Robert J Oppenheimer devote vast resources to ensuring America were the leaders in the race. In 1945, Oppenheimer was ultimately victorious, but what if the bomb had fallen first into the hands of the Soviet Union? Would the weapon have been detonated not over Hiroshima, but Berlin? Would we still have had the Cold War?

What exactly was the Soviet atomic project and how did it fit into the wider race for the bomb taking place during the 1940s?
When nuclear fission was discovered at the end of 1938, Soviet scientists were as excited about the discovery as physicists in other countries. They did work on investigating the possibility of a nuclear fission chain reaction, as either a power reactor or an explosive reaction - a bomb. But in June of 1941, when the Germans invaded the Soviet Union, the work was ended. There were much more immediate tasks at hand because the German armies advanced rapidly and were quickly able to threaten Moscow. Despite this, the Soviet Union did learn about the work going on, initially in Britain and then in the United States, through their intelligence service. Perhaps most importantly they were able to obtain a copy of the MAUD report, which was a classified report investigating the possibility of using uranium to construct a bomb. One of the famous Cambridge Five spies transmitted the report to Moscow in October of 1941, at almost exactly the same time it was being briefed to President Roosevelt in Washington DC. So the Soviet Union was on a par with the US in terms of scientific knowledge regarding an atomic weapon. However, while the report helped to speed up the Manhattan Project it was largely ignored by the Soviet Union. Lavrentiy Beria, who was head of Soviet intelligence, feared that it was a scam designed to distract them. Additionally, the prospect of a bomb in two or three years, which is essentially what the MAUD report stated, didn't seem very interesting when you're desperately trying to defend Moscow against the German attack. However, when intelligence came to Moscow about German work on a potential bomb, Stalin signed the decree setting up a small experimental project of their own.

How much more advanced was the Manhattan Project?
The thing to remember is that although the US entered the war in December 1941, it was not subject to invasion or to bombing in the way the Soviet Union was. By that point the German armies had Leningrad under siege and were even threatening Moscow. Indeed, when Stalin signed the decree setting up the relatively small project it was just as the Battle for Stalingrad was beginning. The scientist who was put in charge, Igor Kurchatov, had to assemble his group at a time when the country was fighting to defend itself. Meanwhile Roosevelt has given authorisation to turn the American research on the bomb into an industrial project. I think we forget that the Manhattan Project employed maybe 120,000 people. So that's the key difference. What you see in the Soviet Union is a pre-industrial project on the bomb, which is constantly receiving espionage concerning the Manhattan Project. The scientists involved were very conscious that they were lagging behind.

What if... THE USSR HAD INVENTED THE ATOMIC BOMB FIRST?

THE PAST

1945
J ROBERT OPPENHEIMER

J Robert Oppenheimer was a gifted physicist, chosen as the scientific director of the American attempt to create an atomic weapon, the Manhattan Project. It was during the war that Oppenheimer became interested in the possibility of nuclear bombs, concerned that Nazi Germany may possibly have already been creating such a weapon. Oppenheimer chose Los Alamos as the site for the project and on 16 July 1945, tested 'Trinity', their first atomic weapon. Oppenheimer was opposed to the bombing of Nagasaki and later, after the war, at the development of the more powerful hydrogen bomb. He was targeted during the 'Red Scare' for supposedly having communist sympathies.

1943
KLAUS FUCHS

Klaus Fuchs was a scientist who in 1943, joined the Manhattan Project. However, Fuchs was also a spy who provided information to the Soviet Union on the development of the American atomic project. He was discovered in 1949 when the United States and Great Britain cracked the famous VENONA codes, used by Soviet spies. Fuchs would be sentenced for 14 years and would then move to East Germany, passing away in 1988. The importance of the information supplied by Fuchs to the Soviet atomic project remains a source of debate. However some argue that his information helped to save the Soviet project precious time.

1943
IGOR KURCHATOV

Igor Kuchatov was the director of the Soviet nuclear programme. Kurchatov was known for wearing a large beard, which he stated would not be cut until the programme succeeded. Kurchatov would later pursue the peaceful use of nuclear technology, becoming fearful of the potential use of atomic weapons. Aware of his own responsibility, he sought to argue against further testing. Despite the success of the Soviet nuclear project, he continued to wear his beard for the remainder of his life.

ABOVE - LEFT
J Robert Oppenheimer, the 'father of the atomic bomb' – would Kurchatov have been given this title instead?

ABOVE - RIGHT
The first successful Soviet atomic test, known as 'first lightning'

So it's likely that it would never have been possible for Kurchatov's group to have overtaken the Manhattan Project any time?
No, I don't think it would have been possible. Just given the conditions of the war. Even if they had decided, let's say before the German attack, to set up the atomic industry to produce the bomb, I doubt it would have been able to survive the subsequent Nazi attack. Due to the timescale, I think the question would be 'we're fighting for our lives, how can we be concerned about a bomb that might appear in two or three years?'

What was the Soviet Union's reaction to the Hiroshima and Nagasaki bombings?
The Soviet Union had very detailed intelligence about the Manhattan Project, but they appear not to have had any intelligence about the plan to use the bomb against Japan. It was a shock for Moscow and a couple of weeks after the bombing of Hiroshima, on 22 August 1945, Stalin signed a decree turning the small but growing Soviet nuclear project into a crash programme to develop the bomb as quickly as possible. They had actually received information about the design of the plutonium bomb, the type dropped on Nagasaki, and it was that design they decided to copy. And so the first Soviet test, which was in August 1949, was actually a copy of the Nagasaki bomb.

What would it have taken for the Soviets to develop the bomb first?
First of all, it would have taken a decision to invest in a very large industrial project to develop the bomb. Additionally, this decision would have to be taken before the summer of 1942, when the United States chose to go ahead with their project and would have had to disregard any cost. Even for the US, that was a major decision taken largely on advice from scientists that not only would this be possible but that maybe the Germans were already building one. In the Soviet Union, there wasn't that great trust between the leadership and the scientists.

The second thing is that, even if they had made that decision, the war would still have changed everything. During the German attack all resources were devoted to the Soviet Union's defence. When Kurchatov was trying to set up his small laboratory, he could hardly get anyone to pay attention to him because everyone was under enormous pressure to fulfil different tasks for weapons production. He even writes a letter complaining about this to Beria.

If the Soviet Union had developed the bomb first, would it have been detonated during the war? Possibly over Germany?
It's certainly possible. The fighting to seize Berlin was ferocious and went on until May 1945 and the use of the bomb might have been regarded as 'helpful' in ending the war. For Britain, strategic bombing was an extremely important part of the way the war was fought, especially after Dunkirk and the British were out of the European continent. But that was not the case with the Soviet

LEFT
A nuclear staffer cleans the first Soviet nuclear bomb, tested in 1949

ABOVE
An article from 1948 demonstrating the fear that the Soviet Union could possibly develop an atomic weapon

Union. The Soviet strategic bombing didn't really play a serious role in their attack on Germany. Their air force was used more in a tactical role to support land forces. However, one could still argue that at the very end of the war, they could have put a bomb on a plane to destroy specific German cities. And that would certainly have been conceivable.

Do you think ultimately we still would have ended up with a Cold War?
Yes, I think so. Because there was still the kind of fundamental ideological difference between the Soviet Union and the United States. The Soviet Union did see victory in the war as another step in the progress towards communism. However, I think the Cold War would have been different because the American monopoly on the bomb or the great lead it had from 1949, made it much easier for the US to make the commitment it did to the post-war defence of Europe. When Eisenhower decided European powers couldn't afford politically or economically to reach the troop levels NATO required, there was always the option to send nuclear weapons to Europe. But I think the fact of the American monopoly initially, and then its superiority in the number of weapons, made certain decisions easier for the US than they would otherwise have been. And so the Cold War could have taken a different shape.

Do you think then we would be feeling the effects now or do you think we'd still be very much in the same world?
I mean, ultimately it would not have made much of a difference because we still would have had two sides with nuclear weapons. The US would still have built up its nuclear forces, after all, it was economically and technologically more powerful than the Soviet Union. Its economy had not been damaged in the same way the Soviet economy was subjected to huge destruction during the war. So I think we still would have got to a point of probably strategic parity and mutual assured destruction, and then it would have been a rivalry of which system was better. So ultimately I don't think that the Soviet Union having more weapons initially would have made that much difference to the eventual outcome.

THE POSSIBILITY

1938

THE NAZI ATOMIC PROJECT
While the Soviet Union most likely could not have developed an atomic weapon before the US, one possibility is that the Nazi project may have been successful before either of them. Nuclear fission was discovered in Berlin in 1938, creating panic in America that the Nazis were on their way to weaponising this discovery. Kurt Diebner was in charge of the project but several scientific miscalculations meant the project lagged behind its American counterpart. The Nazi project relied on expensive heavy water and when the key plant producing this material was destroyed, the project lagged even further behind.

1945

HIROSHIMA AND NAGASAKI
On 6 and 9 August 1945, the United States detonated two atomic bombs over the Japanese cities of Hiroshima and Nagasaki, killing thousands. The next day the Japanese government agreed to a surrender. The decision by President Truman to use atomic weapons, not once but twice, remains a controversial and divisive one. However, if the Soviet Union had been able to develop an atomic weapon first, during World War II, would we have seen the devastating weapons detonated over Europe?

1948-49

NUCLEAR MONOPOLY
The United States' monopoly on nuclear weapons after the end of WWII meant it could rely on the nuclear threat to help defend Europe. Indeed, during the Berlin blockade of 1948-49, a number of B-29 bombers were transferred to the area to demonstrate the willingness of the United States to use nuclear weapons against the Soviet Union if necessary. However, although David J Holloway suggests the US would always have been able to develop the number of weapons necessary for a monopoly, would they have been able to secure this hold on Europe?

What if...

PHILIP II HAD LOST THE BATTLE OF CHAERONEA?

If Philip II of Macedon had lost the Battle of Chaeronea in 338 BCE the history of the entire world may have looked very different

INTERVIEW WITH

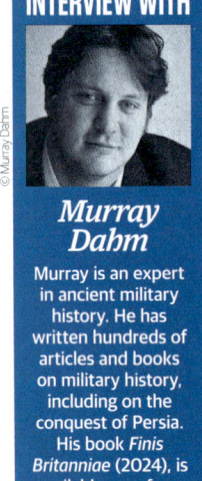

Murray Dahm

Murray is an expert in ancient military history. He has written hundreds of articles and books on military history, including on the conquest of Persia. His book *Finis Britanniae* (2024), is available now from Amberley Publishing.

The Battle of Chaeronea, fought between the forces of Macedon against an alliance of Greek states, in particular Athens and Thebes, in late August 338 BCE, ended in an overwhelming victory for Philip II of Macedon. Thereafter, Macedon dominated the city states of mainland Greece. It was a watershed moment and one of the most significant battles fought in the ancient world. The victory saw Thebes, Athens and other Greek states cowed, and it cleared the way for Macedonian plans to invade the Persian Empire – this would be completed by Philip's son, Alexander, between 334 and 325 BCE.

How significant was the battle and would a different result have changed history that drastically?
The significance of the battle, and Macedon's victory, really cannot be underestimated: it changed the course of ancient Greek history. As such, a different result would have likewise meant a completely different course for the subsequent history of ancient Greece. It is almost inestimable how much things might have changed.

What would a Macedonian defeat have meant?
By 338 BCE, Philip's advance into mainland Greece had been going on for some years. He had already come into conflict with Athens and Thebes. Victory at Chaeronea meant there was no one to stand in his way to take over all the states and impose pro-Macedonian governments. A loss at Chaeronea would have halted this advance and influence, and it may have encouraged more Greek states to join the opposition to Macedon's influence. If Philip and even [his son] Alexander had died in such a defeat then Greece would never have experienced Macedonian domination. The Macedonian Argead royal line would probably have petered out (just as it actually did after Alexander's death in 323 BCE). The Persian Empire would probably not have been invaded, much less conquered, and the entire Hellenistic era – the Macedonian-influenced history of much of the Near East (encompassing modern-day Egypt, Azerbaijan, Turkmenistan, Turkey, Afghanistan, Pakistan and India) – would never have happened. If Philip had died and Alexander lived, there is no guarantee he would have been in a strong position. When he did succeed in 336 BCE his father had enjoyed more success and he had more experience at his side. An unsuccessful new king in 338 BCE could easily have been toppled.

What would it have meant for Greece?
The alliance between Athens and Thebes in 338 BCE was entirely unexpected. Although they had fought beside one another before, they were historic rivals and there was hatred between the two states stretching back more than a century. Athens had been defeated by Thebes in 362 BCE, when Athens sided with Sparta against Theban domination. Now, both sides joined against the common threat of Macedon. Some sources only name these two but others (the orator Demosthenes for instance) names Euboeans, Achaeans, Corinthians,

RIGHT The Philippeion erected at Olympia to commemorate Philip's victory

What if... PHILIP II HAD LOST THE BATTLE OF CHAERONEA?

THE PAST

338 BCE

MACEDON DOMINATES GREECE

Philip's advance to Chaeronea was the culmination of years of work establishing a stable Macedon and then expanding its power. Thessaly fell under his control, and moving into Boeotia was the next logical step. Sparta stayed aloof, but the Greek states led by Athens and Thebes realised that Philip and Macedon posed a threat and joined together to oppose him. This alliance by two erstwhile enemies proved futile: Philip's phalanx and cavalry defeated the Athenians and Thebans at Chaeronea (1,000 Athenians were killed, 2,000 taken prisoner; Thebes lost similar numbers and the 300-strong Sacred Band was wiped out). Philip's crushing victory at Chaeronea ensured he dominated Greece.

334-331 BCE

FALL OF THE PERSIAN EMPIRE

Even after Philip's assassination in October 336 BCE, Macedonian domination continued under his 20-year-old son Alexander, who had had two years of continued success and guidance under his father. He inherited an undefeated army, which he took into Persia to fulfil his father's ambitions. Winning victories in 334 (Granicus), 333 (Issus) and 331 BCE (Gaugamela), Alexander conquered the Persian Empire and took over its governance. He then advanced into Afghanistan and India, creating the largest empire the world had yet seen.

323-330 BCE

THE HELLENISTIC WORLD

Following the death of Alexander the Great in June 323 BCE at only 32, his successors divided up his empire into kingdoms of their own. Despite internecine warfare among them, these kingdoms and the supreme self-confidence which led to their creation (because of the successes of Alexander's conquests) created an unprecedented period of art, literature and science. This dominated the eastern Mediterranean until 30 BCE when the Hellenistic kingdom of Ptolemaic Egypt fell to Rome.

BELOW LEFT The Athenian orator Demosthenes was a leader of the anti-Macedonian faction at Athens

BELOW RIGHT The funerary stele of Panchares, who possibly fell in the Battle of Chaeronea

Thebans, Megarians, Leucadians and Corcyraeans. In many ways the alliance against Macedon's invasion was a unifier, just as the alliance against Persia had been in the fifth century BCE. Given prior Greek history, however, after a combined victory, the Greek states would have probably soon fallen to bickering and fighting among themselves once more. This might have led to another period of Athenian domination or, perhaps, one of Theban domination of the other mainland Greek states.

What about Sparta?

Sparta's influence was already on the wane after two decisive defeats at the hands of the Thebans in 371 BCE (Leuctra) and 362 BCE (Mantinea). What is more, Sparta's manpower and political power had so drastically declined that any recovery was unlikely.

Could Macedon had bounced back from a defeat?

In all probability, a defeat for Macedon at Chaeronea would've been followed by an invasion of Macedon by a combined Athenian and Theban force to ensure that it couldn't [recover]. Even though Thebes was defeated at Chaeronea, in 335 BCE (so only three years later) it revolted from Macedonian control, and Alexander (by then king although he had only been on the throne for a year) took drastic action. He razed Thebes to the ground. This was a frightening precedent – he wiped a city with a vast history from the face of the earth. This made sure that other cities stayed compliant for the remainder of his reign (as soon as he died, they did revolt – but were defeated by Alexander's successors). It is unlikely that the Thebans or Athenians would have destroyed the Macedonian capital Pella but it would have shifted the war to Macedon.

What would it have meant for developments in warfare?

The Macedonian infantry phalanx was inexorable and would remain so – it was the tool used to conquer Greece and then Persia. It then became the dominant infantry formation in the Eastern Mediterranean until the second century BCE. If it had been stopped at Chaeronea, we would not have seen the Macedonian phalanx again – it would not have conquered Persia or become the formation of the Hellenistic kingdoms. In many ways, Greek warfare would have remained conservative: hoplite phalanxes on the Athenian and Theban model. Their arms and armour had remained relatively unchanged since Thebes' victories over Sparta in the 370s and 360s BCE. A victory of those arms at Chaeronea would not have suggested that any change was necessary. The Thebans had been using a deeper formation and this may have become the norm, but other states (like Athens) had retained their age-old depths. Perhaps defeated Macedonians and some Thessalians would have come into mainland Greek warfare as cavalry. This

might have had some influence although what Philip's phalanx showed was that it was the anvil to his cavalry's hammer – this was a tactic Alexander perfected in Persia. Defeat at Chaeronea would have meant that never came to pass.

What else might a Macedonian defeat at Chaeronea have meant?

The tribes and states beyond Macedon (Illyria, Paeonia and the Thracians) had seen significant campaigns by Philip before he turned south into Greece. In this way he had secured his rear and was under no threat from those states when he was preoccupied with Greece. He also had hostages and marriage alliances with these states (Olympias, Alexander's mother, was a princess from Epirus). A Macedonian defeat at Chaeronea (especially if Philip and/or Alexander had been killed) would have probably meant these states would have taken a chance to revolt or invade (either in alliance or singly). Before Philip had come to the throne (358 BCE) they had dominated Macedon so would have looked to reassert that dominance. All of this (and with an Athenian/Theban invasion too) would have meant the Greek states became distracted by their own internal dissent. With Macedon defeated, Athenian orators would have shifted back to Thebes being the common enemy and there would eventually have been another war for control of Greece, probably between Athens and Thebes and their respective allies.

What about Persia?

It is unlikely that Persia would have been invaded had Macedon been defeated at Chaeronea; that victory opened the way for the Macedonian invasion of Persia – planned by Philip and implemented to great effect by Alexander. Other mainland Greek states would have been unlikely to want to dedicate their manpower to such a vast external undertaking. Perhaps an alliance, but it would have been fragile and fraught with divisions. Most Theban and Athenian politicians would have been preoccupied with internal matters, at most reestablishing a Theban or Athenian sphere of influence but one which would not have been so ambitious to consider conquering Babylon or toppling the Persian Empire. Likewise, Persia was in no position to invade Greece again; Artaxerxes III was poisoned at court in 336 BCE and Darius III came to power – he would probably have reigned for years longer if not defeated by Alexander (he was 50 when he died in 330 BCE).

Would there have been any longer-term effects of a Macedonian defeat at Chaeronea

Gosh, where to start? Greece was invaded by rampaging Gallic tribes in 280 BCE led by Brennus, and the Macedonian armies had a very hard time dealing with this invasion. We can't know if a Greece not dominated by Macedon would have fared any better. Perhaps Greece would have fallen under Gallic sway. Likewise, the success of the Macedonian phalanx led to it being called in by the cities of southern Italy against Roman expansion (led by Pyrrhus of Epirus – actually a second cousin to Alexander the Great although he was probably born four years after Alexander's death). Would those cities have appealed to the Greek states with 'normal' hoplite phalanxes? Perhaps. In which case, Rome's conquest of Greece may have been accelerated. Or perhaps Greece (led by Thebes and Athens, or at least an ambitious adventurer from either city) may have had greater influence in Italy – if they had defeated an expanding Rome in the third century BCE, who knows? But that is a 'what if?' for another day!

BELOW
Macedonian King Philip II was the mastermind behind the victory at Chaeronea

BOTTOM
Alexander commanded the cavalry on his father's left wing at the age of just 18

THE POSSIBILITY

338 BCE – UNKNOWN

ATHENS RESURGENT

Athens, along with Thebes, was the leader of the alliance against Macedon at Chaeronea. If the alliance had won, Athens would have been ideally placed as the saviour of Greece to reinvigorate its domination of Greece and the Aegean. Although we admire Athens for its history as it is, it may have been even greater if it had come to dominate Greece from the fourth century BCE onwards. Athenian literature, art and architecture may have had a resurgence and we might now see much more of it surviving.

338 BCE – UNKNOWN

THE PERSIAN EMPIRE

If Athens and Thebes had won at Chaeronea, Macedonian forces would not have invaded and conquered the Persian Empire. It might never have fallen and still be with us. It would not have been divided between Alexander's successors and probably not have splintered as it did into various entities, eventually to become the Parthian Empire. If there was no Parthian Empire, the Sasanian Persians would not have eventuated – the Achaemenid Empire might still have held sway throughout the Roman Empire and beyond. The history of the entire Near East could have been very different if Macedon had lost the Battle of Chaeronea.

338-264 BCE

A GREEK ROMAN EMPIRE

It's hard to imagine the world without the Roman Empire as it was. Yet the domino effect of a different result at Chaeronea might have meant it was Thebes and Athens that came to the aid of the Italian cities against Roman expansion, not Pyrrhus of Epirus. If the Greeks were not looking east, they may have looked west – to Magna Graeca (Italy) and beyond. Sicily and southern Italy already had strong links to Greece. If mainland Greece was strong and confident they could have stopped Roman expansion, even expanded their Italian domains and conquered Rome. Imagine if the Roman Empire as we know it was Greek not Roman – the world would have looked very different with a Greek Empire and the Achaemenid Persian Empire still in place.

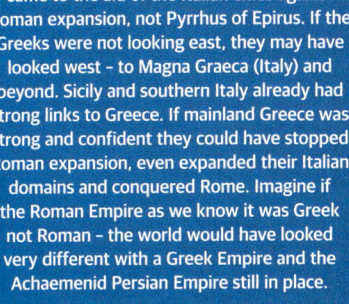

What if...

THE DUNKIRK EVACUATION HAD FAILED?

In 1940 a vast rescue operation miraculously saved the majority of Britain's army, but what would failure have meant in the war against the Nazis?

INTERVIEW WITH

Joshua Levine

Joshua Levine practised as a barrister before becoming an actor and writer. He has written several books on the subject of the two World Wars and served as the historical consultant on the 2017 film *Dunkirk*.

Between 26 May and 4 June 1940, a vast operation took place to rescue thousands of British troops from northern France. The Germans' rapid advance through the difficult and hilly terrain of the Ardennes had outflanked the British forces. Realising that a continued attack would be hopeless, the British launched Operation Dynamo, a huge endeavour to rescue as many troops as possible. The improvised evacuation, involving hundreds of navy and civilian vessels, was nothing short of a miracle. It kept Britain in the war and paved the way for the eventual defeat of Nazi Germany. Yet the success of the operation was on a knife-edge - how might the future of both Britain and WWII have looked had it failed?

What happened leading up to the evacuation of troops at Dunkirk? Why was it necessary?

The British Expeditionary Force arrived in France at the beginning of the war and the expectation was that there would be a confrontation. The Germans, it was believed, would be attacking through Belgium and, initially, the British Expeditionary Force wasn't allowed to advance into Belgium - the Belgians were remaining neutral because they didn't want to provoke the Germans. When the German attack arrived, in May 1940, it came in Belgium as expected, and the British duly moved forward to the River Dyle, where the two sides met. What was expected was a standoff with two armies facing each other across a series of trenches, much like the previous war. But the Germans were simultaneously mounting another attack further south. They did not attack along the Maginot Line, a series of heavily fortified defences built along their border with France. Instead, the Germans launched a daring attack through the Ardennes, a hilly, forested area that was not considered ideal at all for tanks. The area was barely defended and the Germans moved quickly through it. By 20 May, German tanks had reached the French coast. After little more than a week, the Germans had almost surrounded the British Expeditionary Force.

Can you explain the plan for the Dunkirk evacuation?

Basically, there was no plan! It was never anticipated that the army would need rescuing. The evacuation was improvised by Admiral Bertram Ramsay from Dover Castle, where he could literally see across to the French coast. The initial idea was to bring soldiers back from Dunkirk harbour. Ships would be sent directly into the harbour but the Luftwaffe quickly put it out of action. And this is where improvisation reached its height. If you can't lift people from the harbour, what can you do? Well, there's the 10 miles of shallow beaches stretching from France into Belgium. In theory, people could be taken directly off the beaches, but the problem was that the bigger naval and transport ships couldn't get close enough - so initiative was needed. For example, the Royal Engineers used discarded lorries and drove them out into the water, where they were tethered together and a walkway built on top allowing them

RIGHT
Admiral Bertram Ramsay (left), who organised the evacuation, watches Allied aircraft over the Normandy coast in 1944

What if...
THE DUNKIRK EVACUATION HAD FAILED?

What if... THE DUNKIRK EVACUATION HAD FAILED?

THE PAST

1940
HITLER'S HALT ORDER

Just as his troops were ready to move onto the beaches at Dunkirk, Adolf Hitler gave the order for them to halt the advance and left the attack to the Luftwaffe. For years this order has generated controversy. It was suspected for a long time that it might have been given out of a sense of mercy and that Hitler suspected a show of force would now push Britain into making peace. However, Hermann Göring insisted the Luftwaffe be given the honour of finishing off the British Army. Hitler relented and halted the movement of the Panzers outside Dunkirk. Partly this was due to tank losses and the worry this could leave the left flank of the advance vulnerable. This decision would give the British troops valuable time to stage the evacuation.

1912-40
FROM THE TITANIC TO DUNKIRK

One of the men who captained a 'little ship' during the evacuation of British troops at Dunkirk was Charles Lightoller, the surviving second officer of the Titanic, which had sunk in 1912. Lightoller survived the sinking when, as the ship plunged under water, he found himself trapped but was saved when a boiler explosion in the bowels of the ship released a blast of hot air that pushed him to the surface. He then stood on top of an upturned lifeboat with some other surviving passengers, constantly shifting their weight so as not to capsize the little boat, until they were rescued. Pictured here with his son, who also assisted in the evacuation, the 66-year-old Lightoller managed to rescue some 130 British soldiers from the beaches of Dunkirk in his 58ft private motor yacht, The Sundowner. Lightoller would live out the rest of his days running a small boatyard and constructing boats for the river police. In 1952 he would pass away of heart disease.

---

to be used as makeshift jetties. And a lot of smaller boats and ships were needed to lift people off the beaches, so plenty of boat owners around southern England found that their boats were suddenly whisked away. For me, the most impressive improvisation was by a man called Captain William Tennant, who was the senior naval officer ashore in Dunkirk. When he got there on 27 May he realised something had to be done to get people off in larger numbers, because significant numbers of soldiers were starting to arrive inside the Dunkirk perimeter. Captain Tennant spotted the large East Mole; this was a mile-long breakwater, it wasn't a jetty. Ships never came alongside it. But Tennant brought a huge ferry alongside and soldiers found ways to clamber on board. It worked brilliantly.

How integral were the 'little ships' to the evacuation?

There is an idea that ordinary people got in their private little motor boats and came over to Dunkirk, and to some small extent that did happen. A man called Charles Lightoller, who had been the senior surviving officer on board the Titanic, took his own little boat across. But for the most part these 'little ships' were requisitioned in a hurry by the Royal Navy and a lot of their owners thought they had been stolen. As a result, there were civil actions against the Navy for people who lost their boats that carried on for years afterwards! These little ships started arriving in large numbers on 30 May. However, it should be remembered that these ships were, for the most part, not taking people back to England but carrying them from the shore to the larger ships. Their primary role was to ferry people off the beaches.

Could the evacuation have failed?

There was every chance it could have failed. Churchill initially hoped that 30,000 soldiers would get away and in the end 338,000 made it off the beaches. There were an incredible number of things which allowed people to escape. Firstly, there was the successful defence of the roads to Dunkirk and then the defence of the perimeter around Dunkirk by both British and French troops – many of whom were sacrificing themselves for the greater good. Then there was the generally calm sea and the frequent cloud cover. These were strokes of luck, as was the infamous 'Halt Order' that stopped German tanks in their tracks for several crucial days. A little-known scientific process known as 'degaussing' kept hundreds of ships safe from German magnetic mines. You've got the efforts of the Royal Navy and the Merchant Navy, and the work of the little ships. People often forget the work being done by the Royal Air Force. All of these things came together. They're all immensely important and without one or more of them it could all have been different.

If Dunkirk had failed what could the effect on the war have been?

Britain would have almost certainly been forced to seek terms with Germany. Lord Halifax was keen to pursue some kind of negotiation. If Britain had made peace, it would have become – as Churchill said at the time – a slave state. It would

BELOW
Stranded troops on the beaches at Dunkirk during the evacuation in 1940

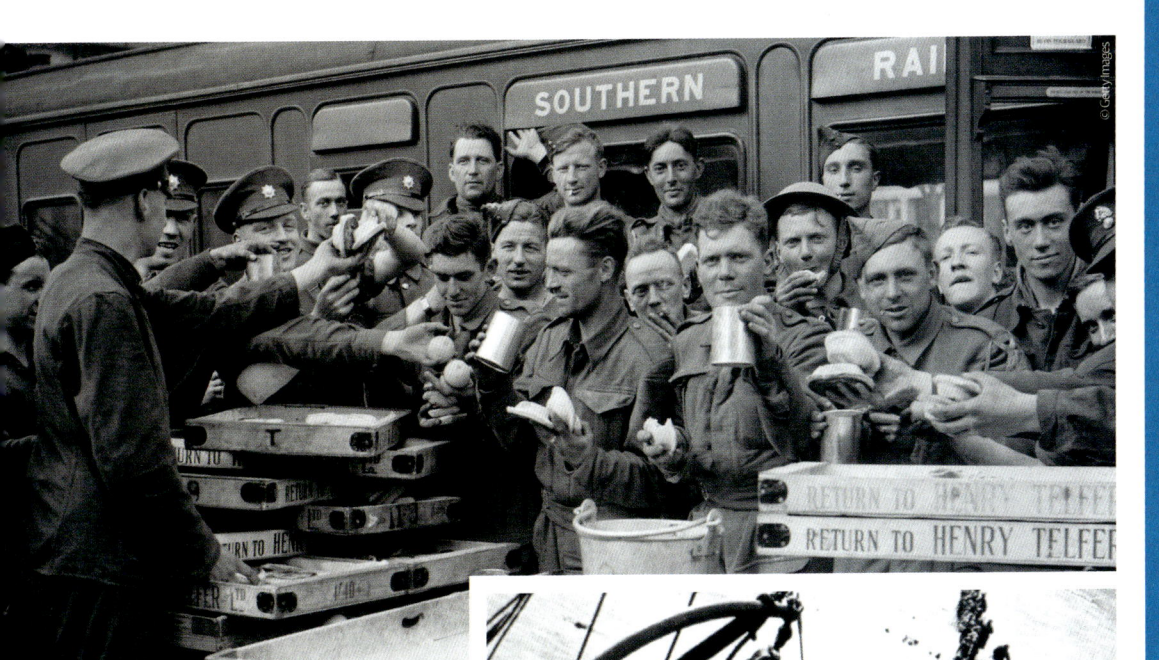

have meant that the war as we know it wouldn't have taken place. Without Britain to preserve freedom and the rule of law then the norms of Nazi Germany would simply have bled right across Europe. Would America still have entered the war? Where would the second front have come from without Britain as a base to get back into Europe? Would Europe have ever been liberated? In America there's a tendency to think of Dunkirk as a sort of parochial little British story that took place before the Americans and the Russians got involved and the real war started. And that's not right. The influence of Dunkirk on the world in which we live is beyond imagination.

What could the failure of the evacuation have meant to Britain?
The evacuation gave rise to an idea known as 'Dunkirk Spirit' which is still bandied about constantly. But in the summer of 1940 it was real and it was organic. The soldiers came home and most were embarrassed. They thought of themselves as the remnants of a battered army, so they were amazed to be treated as heroes by civilians. People were buying them drinks in pubs and slapping them on the back. Families were happy that their sons, brothers and husbands had come home but also they were just relieved that Britain hadn't lost the war. That relief gave rise to a spontaneous release of emotion. Mass Observation reports from the time said that this sudden release of feeling after Dunkirk would rouse the nation. In the immediate aftermath of the evacuation, politicians in the Cabinet started talking about war aims and what they wanted Britain to be like after the war. *The Times* published an editorial saying British life should no longer be based on privilege but on democracy and freedom. Factory output increased massively. I believe Dunkirk was a turning point that led to the post-war social national overhaul. This is what eventually led to the NHS, free education, to all these measures which grew out of the war. The post-war consensus of making life better for people was kickstarted by Dunkirk and had this not happened, I think it's very possible that these post-war measures would not have come about.

TOP
Evacuated troops arrive at Addison Road station and enjoy refreshments

ABOVE
Troops wade into the water to board rescue ships

THE POSSIBILITY

1940

PEACE WITH GERMANY?
Had the Dunkirk evacuation failed and almost the entirety of the British Expeditionary Force been captured in France, then it is more than likely that Britain would have been forced to sue for peace with Nazi Germany. Some in the British Government, such as Lord Halifax, had seen this as a viable option and it was during the May 1940 Cabinet Crisis that he pushed for this. Following the crisis, Halifax found himself in America as Churchill's ambassador. If Operation Dynamo had failed, would this plan have become a reality?

1945

NO SOCIAL REFORMS?
Following the end of the war, it was not Winston Churchill whom the British public chose to lead them but Labour's Clement Attlee, whose programme of social reforms remains influential to this day. The National Insurance Act (1946) introduced social security, and nationalisation acts of coal (1946), electricity and transport (1947) nationalised key parts of British industry. The Children's Act of 1948 introduced a comprehensive child care system for orphaned and poor children. Arguably the most progressive British government ever, Attlee's five-year term is one whose positive effects we are still feeling today. As Joshua Levine describes, without Dunkirk these reforms may have never have occurred.

1948

NO NHS?
Perhaps the most important of Attlee's reforms was the creation of the National Health Service (NHS), which came into being in 1948. Some of the origins of the NHS originate directly following the Dunkirk evacuation, with William Beveridge's 1942 report that outlined societal problems to be faced following the end of the war. Attlee's Health Minister, Aneurin Bevan, expressed the desire that the new health system should be based on three major principles. Firstly that it be for everyone, secondly that it be free, and finally that it would be based on need and not ability to pay.

What if...

POMPEY HAD DEFEATED JULIUS CAESAR?

How the outcome of one battle would have changed the history of the Roman Empire as we know it

INTERVIEW WITH

Dr Simon Elliott

Dr Elliott is a bestselling author, historian, archaeologist, broadcaster, and Honorary Research Fellow at the University of Kent. His books include *Roman Legionaries*, *Julius Caesar: Rome's Greatest Warlord* and *Roman Conquests: Britain*.

Former political allies, and even allied through marriage, Julius Caesar and Pompey faced each other across a battlefield at Pharsalus in Greece, in 48 BCE, as deadly enemies. Political convenience had turned to dust and the outcome of this battle would determine the fate of both men, and the future of Rome and its influence in the world.

Was it inevitable that Pompey and Caesar would come to blows? How different were they, and was Pompey as ambitious as Caesar?
Yes, absolutely they would have come to blows. Both were the leading protagonists in their generation for the two main political factions in Roman politics. These were the optimates who were reactionary and pro-Senate, and the populares who were in favour of reform and supported by the lower orders of the Roman aristocracy and society. They were both the latest incumbents to champion their respective causes, following on from Lucius Cornelius Sulla and Gaius Marius in the preceding generation.

While both men were ambitious, it was Caesar who definitely had the edge. All political leaders of the Roman Republic were in effect independent warlords, and shared to a greater or lesser degree a number of leadership traits. These included personal bravery; the ability to be brutal when necessary; strategic and tactical prowess; the ability to communicate with audiences high and low; that most Roman of traits, grit, which meant they kept coming back; the charisma to inspire on a large scale; and decisiveness. Caesar was the only one who had them all, and because of this he was the warlord who was the most constantly, and conspicuously, successful. That is why I believe he was Rome's greatest warlord.

Had Caesar been captured what would Pompey's options have been? And his most likely course of action?
That is a very good question. I believe Pompey would have liked to be merciful to his rival. The destruction of a political opponent was a grave matter in the world of Republican Rome. Note, for example, Caesar's fury when he learnt that Pompey had been beheaded on arrival in Ptolemaic Egypt after fleeing the defeat at Pharsalus. However, on the eve of that battle Pompey knew he had been bested by the arriviste Caesar, the latter in particular making his name in his dramatic and sanguineous conquests of Gaul. Caesar's aggressive strategy against the optimates certainly put his rivals on the back foot. Further, while Caesar was far and away the leading populares champion, Pompey was more of a first among equals. This proved to be the case after his death when the optimates cause continued in further civil war until 45 BCE. Therefore, I think Pompey's hands would have been tied. Much as he would

RIGHT
Julius Caesar would become a dictator whose dynasty started an empire

RIGHT-INSET
Pompey The Great was a stalwart of the Republic

What if...
POMPEY HAD DEFEATED JULIUS CAESAR?

What if... POMPEY HAD DEFEATED JULIUS CAESAR?

THE PAST

60s & 50s BCE

DRIVEN BY AMBITION
Both Caesar and Pompey were successful, seasoned campaigners in battle, and that would both bring them together and drive them apart. Success in war had gained them wealth and the respect of the people, which in turn gave them the platform for the political ambition and eventually rivalry that was to drive them towards their individual fate.

60-53 BCE

THE TRIUMVIRATE
To further their own ends within the Senate, Caesar and Pompey formed a private alliance with the fabulously wealthy Marcus Crassus, known to us as the First Triumvirate (60-53 BCE). Through such political manoeuvring, Caesar became Consul and as a result all three increased their power and influence. But the alliance was a troubled one and following the death of Crassus in a military campaign, plus the death of Julia (Caesar's daughter and Pompey's wife) relations between the two remaining allies were stretched to the limit and the triumvirate came to an end.

49 BCE

CAESAR CROSSES THE RUBICON
Roman law forbade any military leader from crossing into Italy with a standing army. Following further successful military campaigns, in 49 BCE Caesar took the ultimate step of crossing the Rubicon River, which formed the northern boundary of Italian territory, without disbanding his legions, in defiance of the Senate. It was an open act of treason from Caesar, resulting in civil war and leading Caesar and Pompey to the inevitable clash at the Battle of Pharsalus.

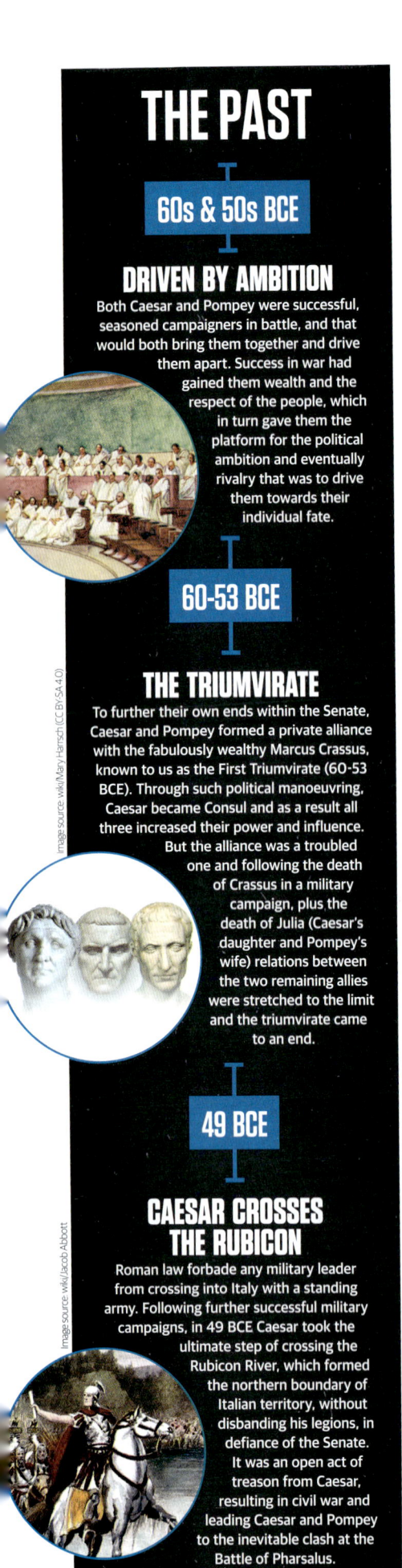

have liked to have kept Caesar alive, perhaps as an exile, he knew that his fellow optimates expected his opponent to be killed - an event that would have secured victory for the optimates.

What role would Pompey have seen for himself in Rome and how would he have secured it?
If Pompey had defeated Caesar I don't believe he would have had the option of setting himself up as a dictator for life as Caesar had done, given he was the leading optimates rather than their actual - individual - leader. He would have championed a return to the normal Republican Roman status quo, with annual elections for twin consuls, though of course occasionally he himself would have put himself forward as one!

What would a Pompey victory have meant for the likes of Mark Antony, Cleopatra and Octavian? And what effect would this have on history?
They would have become footnotes in history. Mark Antony, while successful in the final stages of the 1st century BCE civil wars in Rome, was no Caesar. Though a skilful political operator, he would likely have perished soon after Caesar's defeat. Meanwhile the optimates broadly favoured Cleopatra VII's rival for political power in Alexandria, her brother Ptolemy XIII. While unquestionably a powerful ruler in her own right, without Caesar and later Antony championing her cause Cleopatra would most likely have been just another ruler in the long line of squabbling Ptolemaic monarchs. Similarly,

ABOVE Pompey's alliance with Ptolemy XIII could have grown even stronger

BELOW The Battle of Pharsalus saw Julius Caesar defeat Pompey the Great

Octavian owed his later elevation to Caesar championing him as the latter reached the ascendancy of his domination of Roman political life. Without that elevation, and given his family association with Caesar and the populares, he again would most likely have either been killed or disappeared into obscurity.

Would the influence of the Roman world in size and culture have been different after a Pompey victory? If so, how?
Not necessarily. By the time of Pharsalus, Rome was easily the dominant power in the western and eastern Mediterranean worlds, with no symmetrical opponent left except perhaps the Parthians in the east. To that end, Rome was already far down the road of assimilating Greek, Egyptian and Punic culture into its own way of life. Furthermore, even if Caesar had been defeated, his optimates

opponents would still have had the same desire to expand Roman influence even further afield.

Would Rome have still become an Empire if Pompey had won?
Possibly, but later. While the Republic would most likely have continued in the short term, as I have explained, Rome was now the conqueror of all it surveyed. Therefore, any significant conflict would most likely have come in a new round of civil wars, though perhaps somewhat later than actually happened. In that context, there is no reason to think another populares strongman might have emerged to later take on Caesar's mantle of reform for the Republic. A victory then for this warlord would then perhaps, as happened in reality, have set in place the path to Empire.

What three specific historical events would have been very different because of a Pompey victory over Caesar? And how may subsequent history have changed because of them?
The Roman Empire would not have come into being at the time and in the way it did, even if later it might have appeared in some form. That would then have had a direct impact on the development of the various political entities geographically surrounding the world of Rome, whether the Germans north of the Danube, Parthians in the east, Numidians in North Africa, or Spaniards in the remaining unconquered regions of the Iberian Peninsula. Next, it was Caesar who put Britain on the Roman map with his two incursions in 55 BCE and 54 BCE. Without his interest there perhaps Roman engagement may have withered, instead of Augustus planning though cancelling three invasions, Caligula likewise cancelling one, and ultimately Claudius invading in force in 43 CE to set up the province of Britannia. Finally, Caesar has been the inspiration for political and military leaders ever since his dramatic Icarus-like ascent and ultimate demise. In modern times we still style autocratic leaders in his image, for example think Slavic Tsars and German Kaisers. Perhaps a failure on his part at Pharsalus might have encouraged those who sought (and seek) power at the end of the sword to think again. But probably not!

BELOW
Caesar's ally Mark Antony may not have survived a Pompey victory

THE POSSIBILITY

55-54 BCE

ROMAN BRITAIN WIPED FROM HISTORY?
Caesar's minor explorations of Britain and his interest in expanding into the country may well have died with him at Pharsalus. With the possibility of Pompey taking Roman expansion in a completely different direction, the unknown territory may well have stayed untouched by Rome. No Hadrian's Wall, no Roman roads, no villas and no Roman culture that was to have a lasting effect on the development of the British people.

69-30 BCE

CLEOPATRA WHO?
As the victor, rather than being killed in Egypt at the orders of Ptolemy, Pompey may have strengthened their alliance. It would mean a very different future for Ptolemy's sister and joint ruler, Cleopatra. As Ptolemy's enemy she would be Pompey's enemy, ending in obscurity or death. Her mythical beauty would never have been celebrated, and her famous love affair (and child) with Caesar and later Mark Antony, ending in her suicide, would never have happened.

44 BCE

A VERY DIFFERENT DYNASTY
Julius Caesar was the first of a new order in Rome with ultimate power in the hands of one man. Despite his assassination and the consequent civil war his line endured through his adopted son Octavian (Caesar Augustus). But Pompey was much more of a republican, and a dynastic dictatorship through a line of emperors may possibly never have happened. There would be no Augustus, Tiberius, Caligula or Claudius. Whether there had been an emperor or a republic, events would've shaped the empire very differently.

What if...

THE FRANKS HAD LOST THE BATTLE OF TOURS?

With a Muslim success at Tours, the culture, religion and power of the Arab world could reach deeper into Europe than ever before

INTERVIEW WITH

Professor James T Palmer

Professor James T Palmer is an early medieval historian at the University of St Andrews. His book *Merovingians Worlds* was published by Cambridge University Press in 2024.

Having established a strong Islamic foothold in the Iberian Peninsula, aspirations of territory and power north of the Pyrenees was perhaps a logical step to take. But the region between Poitiers and Tours was not just a step, it was a giant leap, and a huge gamble. Standing in the way of the Muslim forces, Charles Martel has historically been depicted as the embodiment of staunch Christian fortitude, faith, and resilience to repel the invader and destroy his ambitions. Victory would preserve both his religion and his people. Failure would unlock the gates of France to dominance by the Arab world and change the face of Europe forever.

What next steps would the Umayyad Caliphate need to take to consolidate a victory at Tours?
Marching an army as far north from Arab-controlled Spain as Tours was a bit of a wild move. The Arab governor, 'Abd al-Rahman, was trying to take advantage of conflict between Charles Martel and the Duke of Aquitaine at a time when the King of the Franks in Paris had little authority. Bold moves had worked before in the Arab conquests of the Levant and North Africa. Consolidation there always involved targeting administrative centres and working with local populations to keep administration functioning. In the Frankish Kingdom, that would have meant targeting Paris next and hoping that alliances could be forged quickly with nobles who were feeling mercenary or who were tired of the weaknesses of the Merovingian Frankish kings – a dynasty that hadn't produced a dynamic figurehead in decades. The Arabs had presented themselves as a positive change to nobles in Visigothic Spain when they conquered the region in 711 and that had made for a relatively bloodless process.

The safer alternative for 'Abd al-Rahman would have been to focus on commanding the southern cities of Toulouse and Narbonne. These had once formed the core of the Visigothic Kingdom of Aquitaine, crushed by the Franks in 507. Even 200 years later, people in Narbonne still resisted rule by northerners like Charles Martel. Indeed, after the Battle of Tours, Charles had to fight a major campaign in 737 because people in Provence allied with more Arabs against him. If 'Abd al-Rahman had tried a more patient approach, he could have found people in the south willing to support him against perceived northern oppression.

What would be the potential social and cultural impacts for the region following a Muslim victory?
Culturally, one of the biggest changes would be that the Latin West connected to more advanced philosophy and science earlier. Arab intellectuals embraced and developed complex Greek thought long lost to the Latins. With the adoption of Arabic as an extra learned language, the Franks could have been part of that.

Many Franks would have remained Christian. In Spain and elsewhere, Christians and Jews paid the *jizya* tax to be allowed to keep their observances. The downside was that they then had

RIGHT
The Battle of Tours would prove decisive for the Frankish Kingdom, and Europe

What if...
THE FRANKS HAD LOST THE BATTLE OF TOURS?

"SOMEONE GET THESE LADS AN ASTROLABE"

47

What if... THE FRANKS HAD LOST THE BATTLE OF TOURS?

THE PAST

711
ISLAM COMES TO IBERIA

The trigger for Muslim presence in the Iberian Peninsula was either an appeal for help by the Christian Chief, Julian, to fight the tyrannical Visigoth King Roderick, or the invasion was simply driven by the desire to expand Islamic territory and influence. Either way, the Muslim governor of North Africa, Musa ibn Nusayr, sent troops and swiftly overcame and defeated the Visigoth army, killing King Roderick. The Visigoth rulers had been deeply unpopular, and by offering generous surrender terms, the Muslim (or Moorish) armies were soon in control of most of Spain and Portugal.

481-731 CE
INFIGHTING AND DIVISION

From the aftermath of the Roman Empire, the Germanic tribes merged into a single Frankish empire under Clovis, and the Merovingian Dynasty was born. The Merovingian court was violent and unstable. From the uncertainty a new title of authority emerged – Mayor of the Palace. Upon the death of one of these mayors, Pippin II, his illegitimate son Charles (Martel) emerged as a major contender. But he had to fight, and fight hard, overcoming several rebellions through numerous military campaigns across the Frankish regions – providing invaluable experience and skill in battle and diplomacy.

732
MAKE OR BREAK FOR MARTEL

Muslim leader 'Abd al-Rahman had crossed the Pyrenees and defeated the forces of Eudes of Aquitaine at Bayonne and Bordeaux. Eudes was no friend of Charles Martel, but in his desperation, he asked for help against the Islamic forces. While the forces sacked Bordeaux, the Franks assembled an army. Meeting somewhere between Poitiers and Tours, it is believed the Frankish infantry held strong against the Muslim cavalry, turning the tide of battle in their favour. A raid by the Franks on 'Abd al Rahman's supply camp dispersed and fractured the Islamic army and they retreated. 'Abd al-Rahman was killed in the battle.

ABOVE-LEFT
Moorish architecture could have been widespread throughout Europe

ABOVE-RIGHT
The Pyrenees were no barrier to the invading armies of Islam

BELOW
Paris could have had its own version of the Alhambra Palace

reduced rights, fewer opportunities for advancement, and paid more tax.

Matters might have been more contentious in the parts of the Frankish Kingdom that are in what is now Germany, Belgium and the Netherlands. The Franks there had long felt themselves to be politically and culturally distinct from the royal heartlands around Paris. A new Arab regime in Paris may have strengthened that sense of difference and encouraged the formation of a German kingdom a century earlier than actually happened. Moreover, in the furthest northern and eastern parts, there were frontiers with pagan peoples who could not pay the *jizya* as they were not peoples of the Book. Pagan religions in these parts may have seen a resurgence in the face of a weak Christian leadership and the threat of Muslim conquest – and with that, more war would have followed.

What consequences would a defeat have for Charles Martel himself?
If Charles had survived, he would have retreated to the Rhineland to regroup. He had faced military setbacks before and hadn't come to dominate the Frankish Kingdom by giving up. From Cologne, Charles could have led a fresh alliance of Germanic-speaking regions against the Arabs. He had already made progress in uniting German territories by marrying the niece of the Duke of Bavaria, a move that bound the two most powerful families in the east together.

Charles Martel's eldest two children from his first marriage were also coming of age and were well-placed to continue any fight. In real life the younger son, Pippin III, proved such an effective campaigner and leader he was elected the first Frankish king of the Carolingian dynasty in 751 – paving the way for his son, Charlemagne, to revive the Western Empire. There potentially was a lot of fight left in the family.

How might other European kingdoms respond and how might their political dynamic have changed?
The reputation of the Franks was long diminished after decades of in-fighting and uninspiring leadership. A similar situation in Spain had meant few neighbours followed affairs there – and most people thought the Arab conquest was probably the Visigoths' own fault. The fate of the Franks, too, would have been seen as a warning about weak and immoral action in the early years.

In Britain and Ireland, there was already a sense of religious superiority. That would only have grown. More English and Irish holy people would have headed to the continent in order to prop up Christianity and possibly to have agitated for non-cooperation with the Arabs. The Arabs would have been too stretched consolidating control of Spain and France to do much more than attempt occasional raids across the water. And if they did, they were about to face great competition: the First Viking Age was only one generation away.

All eyes would have been on the Byzantine Empire. Would they be able to lead some kind of fight back? The Siege of Constantinople in 717-18 had marked the end of a century of defeats and contraction. In practical terms, however, emperors could have done little more than they did in reality: forge alliances with groups across Eastern Europe and Italy.

What would be the impacts practically and reputationally for the Christian Church?

The Christian Church in 732 was deeply divided and inconsistent. Charles Martel's victory actually didn't help in the short term as he used ecclesiastical resources to reward his followers and support his army. A story circulated that, on his death, he was dragged into the pits of Hell by a dragon for his sins! Reformers complained that the Church was too full of noblemen indulging in sex, drinking and hunting. Muslim rule would have impoverished the churches and made it less attractive as an institution to abuse – but it would also have lost even more of its social authority in the process.

The effects on the papacy would have been dire. Charles Martel's victory ultimately enabled the popes to enlist the Franks to defend them from Lombard and Arab assaults. Without a strong patron, the city of Rome would have fallen to one or the other – and probably several times over. The papacy would have been stripped of much of its wealth. Without the Carolingian Empire, it would never have become the influential force it became either. Popes may have stayed little more than bishops of Rome.

ABOVE A depiction of Charles Martel defeating the army of the caliph in 732

BELOW Charles Martel ("the Hammer") would establish the Carolingian dynasty

Other than just land, what would be the valuable gains for the Caliphate by expanding into Frankish territory, and what could have been its potential ambitions?

The Frankish Kingdom was the strongest of the post-Roman territories. Conquering it would have been an impressive achievement. For 'Abd al-Rahman, this could have offered the opportunity to set up his own dynasty in a wealthy land with an administrative infrastructure that could be built up in time. To combine it with Spain and parts of North Africa would have meant he was a truly powerful figure.

And in many respects, Tours was about 'Abd al-Rahman's Western ambitions rather than about the Umayyads. He was not under any orders to invade or raid. The attack was a punt. Córdoba was so far from the caliphal capital of Damascus that direct control was already an unrealistic proposition anyway. Paris would have been too. It was only a matter of time before regional governors would be able to resist the will of the centre. This was proven soon enough. In 747 the 'Abbasid Revolution began, ultimately overthrowing the Umayyads in the East, and leading to the caliphate recentring on Baghdad. Córdoba stayed loyal to the Umayyads and so effectively became independent of the 'Abbasid Caliphate.

THE POSSIBILITY

800 CE

A VIKING EUROPEAN EMPIRE?

Viking raids had already established a network of trade and influence across Europe, stretching from Ireland to Russia. With a real threat of Muslim expansion across France, and possibly further, Christendom could have become more fractured and plummet into crisis. While resources were focused on the perceived threat from the Arab Caliphate in the south, the Vikings could have seized the opportunity to make territorial gains from the north, expanding their trade, boosting their hordes of silver, and even setting down roots to establish legitimate political power.

1096 CE ONWARDS

CRUSADES CANCELLED

Should more of Europe had fallen under Arab influence, then any call to arms by the Christian church to attack the Holy Land may well have fallen on deaf ears. Not only could the influence of the papacy have been somewhat reduced by Muslim success, but to defeat Muslim forces in the East would be meaningless if you left your homeland open and vulnerable to the Arab forces in the West. Much of Western Europe may have become more closely integrated with North Africa and the Middle East and with it proven greater religious plurality, albeit at a price. Political and religious battle lines in medieval history would have been very different.

PRE 1400 CE

A LIGHT BULB MOMENT FOR EUROPE

With the spread of Islamic control and influence throughout Europe, there is the possibility that greater access to the writings and knowledge of Greek and Arab philosophy and scientific thought would have stimulated learning among European scholars. Centuries before the Renaissance of Da Vinci and Michelangelo, there could have been an acceleration in creative thought in the arts and architecture. European society could have seen advances in creative city planning, and mass-produced books potentially available much earlier through developments in printing.

What if...

THE SPANISH EMPIRE HAD TRIED TO INVADE CHINA?

Could a Spanish invasion in the 16th century have resulted in a war with China?

INTERVIEW WITH

Alexander Samson

Professor Alexander Samson is a professor of Early Modern Studies at University College London. He is the author of *Mary and Philip: The Marriage of Tudor England and Habsburg Spain* (Manchester University Press, 2021).

In the late 16th century, plans were floated throughout the increasingly powerful Spanish Empire for a possible conquest of China. Many of those in the recently acquired Spanish territory of Manila, including governor Francisco de Sande, were in favour of using the Philippines to stage such an attack. Were it not for the reluctance on the part of Philip II, who was occupied with threats in Europe, perhaps an invasion would have been launched. But could it have been successful? Or would it have resulted in disaster?

Why did the Spanish Empire contemplate invading China?
At the very beginning of the 16th century, the Spanish were competing with the Portuguese and wanted to seize a port similar to Macau. Spain's initial interest in China arose from early contacts between the Portuguese and Chinese. These began around 1511 in Malacca, in modern-day Malaysia, a city of perhaps 100,000 inhabitants which the Portuguese had seized from Sultan Mahmud Shah. The first European diplomatic mission departed from this Portuguese colony for the Middle Kingdom in 1517, reaching Canton before eventually setting out for Peking in 1520, where the envoys were imprisoned and then executed. The surviving ships from Ferdinand Magellan's voyage passed through the Moluccas, or Spice Islands, (known today as the Maluku Islands) in 1521, which had been discovered by the Portuguese in 1512. Very little was known about China in the West, in contrast to the Americas, until the second half of the 16th century, although there are some Portuguese manuscript sources from as early as 1524. The notion of armed incursion, the seizure of a port or of the whole province of Canton, was mooted in these accounts. They also described an "effeminate" Chinese population exploited and tyrannised by mandarins, with a defective military. The Portuguese attempted to establish themselves from the 1520s in Macau, but suffered a series of naval defeats, with the Chinese reverse-engineering and then mass-producing the canon and firearms they had captured, neutralising any military advantage Europeans may have possessed. Eventually they signed a treaty and leased Macau to the Portuguese in 1557 in exchange for silver, an arrangement that lasted until 1999.

Were there actual plans in place?
Spanish fantasies of an invasion of China, intending to duplicate what they had done in Mesoamerica [an historical region comprising the southern part of North America and almost the entirety of Central America], began to take more concrete form following the first successful trans-Pacific voyage led by Andrés de Urdaneta, which reached Acapulco in 1565. Shortly afterwards in 1571 Miguel López de Legazpi declared

RIGHT
Wokou pirates raided China during the 13th to 15th centuries. Their presence has been described as war by another name by Alexander Samson

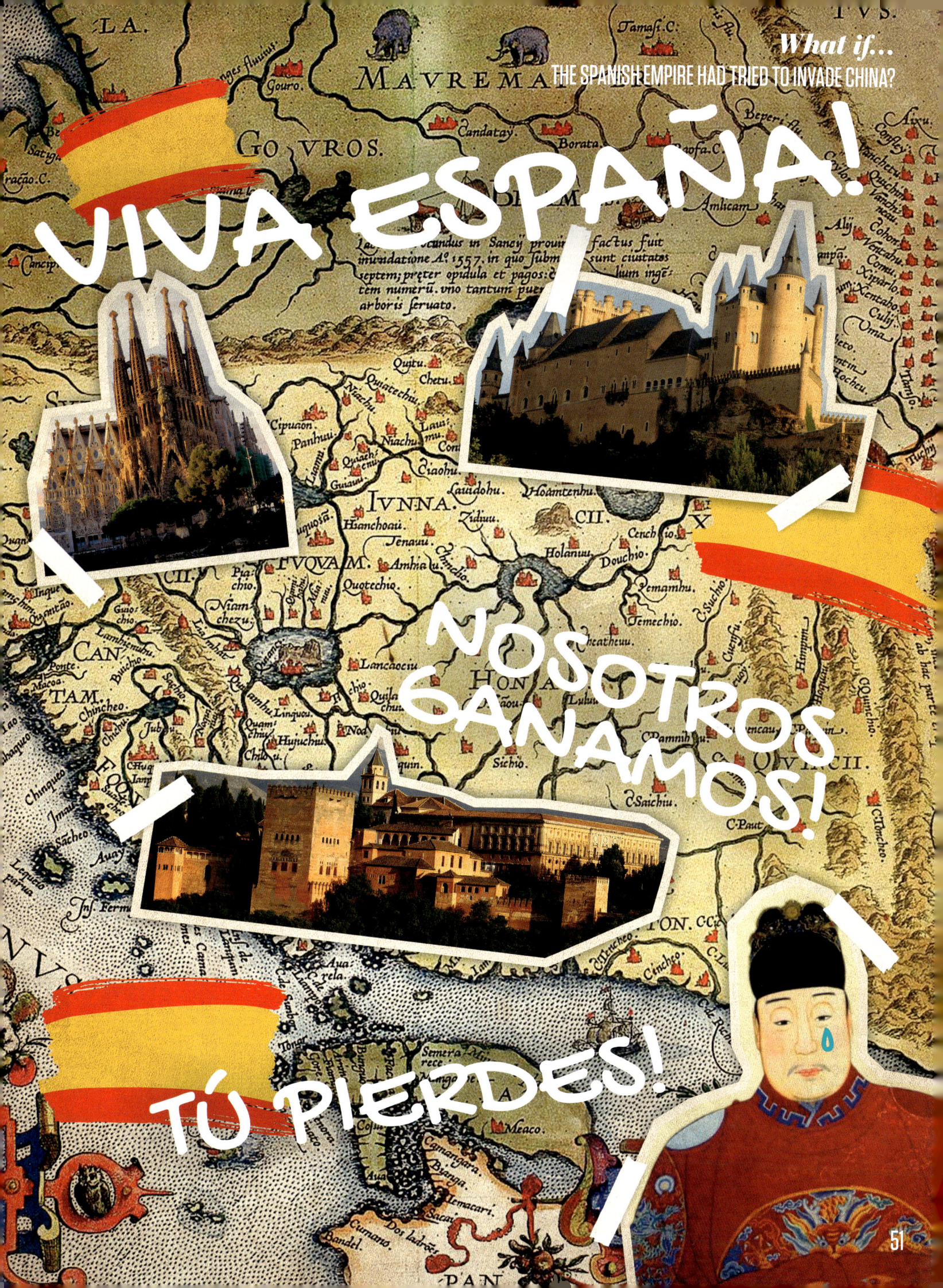

What if...
THE SPANISH EMPIRE HAD TRIED TO INVADE CHINA?

¡VIVA ESPAÑA!

¡NOSOTROS GANAMOS!

¡TÚ PIERDES!

What if... THE SPANISH EMPIRE HAD TRIED TO INVADE CHINA?

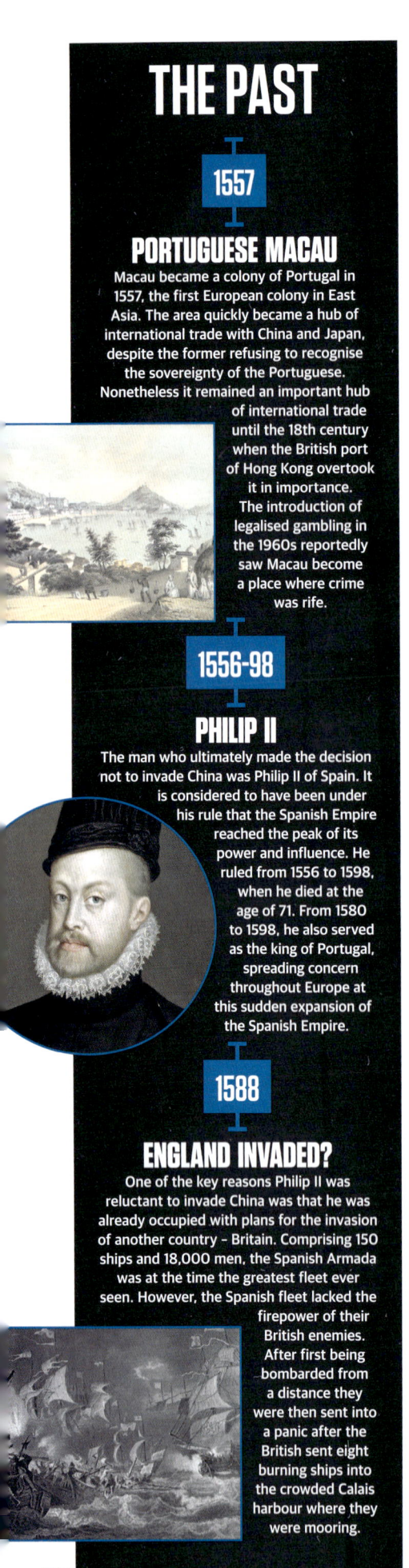

THE PAST

1557
PORTUGUESE MACAU
Macau became a colony of Portugal in 1557, the first European colony in East Asia. The area quickly became a hub of international trade with China and Japan, despite the former refusing to recognise the sovereignty of the Portuguese. Nonetheless it remained an important hub of international trade until the 18th century when the British port of Hong Kong overtook it in importance. The introduction of legalised gambling in the 1960s reportedly saw Macau become a place where crime was rife.

1556-98
PHILIP II
The man who ultimately made the decision not to invade China was Philip II of Spain. It is considered to have been under his rule that the Spanish Empire reached the peak of its power and influence. He ruled from 1556 to 1598, when he died at the age of 71. From 1580 to 1598, he also served as the king of Portugal, spreading concern throughout Europe at this sudden expansion of the Spanish Empire.

1588
ENGLAND INVADED?
One of the key reasons Philip II was reluctant to invade China was that he was already occupied with plans for the invasion of another country – Britain. Comprising 150 ships and 18,000 men, the Spanish Armada was at the time the greatest fleet ever seen. However, the Spanish fleet lacked the firepower of their British enemies. After first being bombarded from a distance they were then sent into a panic after the British sent eight burning ships into the crowded Calais harbour where they were mooring.

Manila a territory of New Spain and from then until the 19th century the Manila galleon was the most significant global trading link. Taking advantage of the fact that the money supply for a quarter of the world's population was silver, Castile had discovered vast reserves of it at Potosí [in modern-day Bolivia] and developed innovative silver amalgamation techniques on top of a difference in the relative value of silver and gold in the Americas and Asia. A Spanish merchant writing in the early 17th century asserted that a given quantity of gold was worth double the amount of silver in China. One of the early evangelists, Martín de Rada, called for an invasion but it was the [Philippines] governor Francisco de Sande who advocated for it most strongly, envisaging the conquest of the kingdom of Taiping with 4,000 men and six galleys. Philip II categorically rejected the idea in 1577, wishing to cultivate friendly relations with the Chinese and considering the sending of an embassy to the Emperor Wanli in 1580. The union of the Iberian crowns between 1580 and 1640 provided a fresh opportunity for the hawks, though, and soon the Jesuit Alonso Sánchez travelled to Madrid to lobby for an invasion. His efforts were thwarted, firstly by news that Matteo Ricci and Michele Ruggieri had won permission in 1585 to settle in Zhaoqing, undermining the argument that the Chinese were preventing evangelisation, and finally with the news of the defeat of the Grand Armada in 1588.

Could it have feasibly worked?
In a word, no. The Spanish were fully aware that, as one commentator put it, China was the greatest kingdom in the world. Its cities were five-times the size of European metropolises and in 1600 its population of around 150 million dwarfed Spain's 8.5 million. The notion that the people were effeminate and corrupt, with a weak military, was largely a comforting fantasy to promote an aggressive stance, but even at their most fully worked out, Spanish plans only ever envisaged the taking of a province. The advanced administrative machinery of the Chinese state may have been bureaucratic but it was also formidable and produced a homogeneity that was not found in Mesoamerica. Similarly the Ming military, even though it was much eroded by the 16th century with its theoretical strength of 3 million soldiers in fact only around 850,000, was still many times larger than any European army in the 16th century. In the wars that saw the change of dynasty in the mid-17th century, the rebel Li Zicheng alone commanded an army of 350,000.

Why did Spain choose not to invade?
Philip II was ultimately preoccupied with problems closer to home, not least Elizabethan England and the revolt of the Dutch Republic from 1565. In terms of logistics, the supply of troops and ships would have taken months to arrive. Most importantly perhaps was the impossibility of command and control, with missives having to make a round trip of at least six months. Information and knowledge of China was sufficiently vague and contradictory to make any prediction of victory highly uncertain. The East Indies was a very different world from Mesoamerica, with a multiplicity of seafaring and trading nations, including Japan, whose merchants got around the ban on direct trade with China by using Manila as a neutral meeting place. Finally, the Habsburg finances would not permit another military commitment, with numerous bankruptcies across his reign.

If the Spanish had invaded China, what would have been some of the immediate effects?
The logistical sophistication of the Chinese administration would have meant that knowledge of these invaders would have travelled quickly to the emperor in Beijing.

BELOW
Macau was a colony of Portugal until 1999. The Spanish wanted a similar piece of territory

ABOVE
Philip II decided against invading China partly because he was preparing for an invasion of England using the Spanish Armada

He would have mustered the forces he was able to, and most likely crushed the insurgents in his territory. But assuming they had established a bridgehead on the Chinese mainland, it seems likely that the various regions, provinces and kingdoms of the empire would have vied to ally themselves with the interlopers in order to dominate other groups. But it is unlikely the country that produced Sun Tzu's *The Art of War* would have been naïve enough to allow themselves to be divided and conquered. The Spanish presence may have precipitated the disintegration of Ming China and brought forward Mongol and Manchurian invasions. Along with banditry and piracy, the Europeans best chance of surviving would have been a long and protracted civil war such as the one that was experienced in the middle of the 17th century. But I suspect they would have been kicked out by a provincial governor before news even arrived at the emperor's court.

Would it have led to retaliation from China or even a possible Chinese invasion of Spain?
No. I think one of the features of life in Southeast Asia during this period was piracy. Piracy was a kind of an endemic problem for the Chinese throughout this period and was essentially a war fought by other means. The Chinese state itself would simply have been too occupied with its own problems, its own economic and social and cultural problems, to focus on any kind of an expansionist agenda.

What would've been the global effects?
This is an interesting counterfactual. There are perhaps two lines one could pursue here. If the Spanish had established themselves, it might have forced disparate forces to ally themselves with each other, unifying the empire in a way that might have prevented its collapse half-a-century later. This might have precipitated a more aggressive and militarised expansionist Chinese state that would have tried harder to dominate the world of the South China Sea, beginning with the expulsion of Spain from the Philippines. This would have disrupted the artery connecting China and Latin America, a flow of silver that precipitated the first age of globalisation. On the other hand, it might have brought forward the war that would see the end of three centuries of the Ming Dynasty, allowing Europeans to integrate themselves into a complex and shifting trading world.

THE POSSIBILITY

16TH CENTURY

THE END OF THE SPANISH COLONIES IN THE PHILIPPINES?

The Philippines were a Spanish colony from 1521, when Ferdinand Magellan first made landfall, until the revolution of 1898. The islands even take their name from Philip II. Had the Spanish chosen to invade China, it is likely that they would have used the Philippines as a possible base from which to stage the attack. Had China retaliated, or some form of war had broken out, would the Philippines have remained under Spanish control for much longer?

1572-1620

CHINA AS A MILITARY FORCE

During the period the Spanish were thinking of invading, Emperor Ming Shenzong (or the Wanli Emperor as he was known) ruled over China. Reported to be something of a recluse he appeared to leave the running of government to others, which resulted in rising corruption. However, despite this it has been argued that he was an effective military leader and the number of available troops was vast compared to those the Spanish could have commanded. It's likely the emperor's forces would have successfully seen off the Spanish.

1368-1644

BREACHING THE GREAT WALL

During the Ming Dynasty, the Great Wall of China was constantly strengthened and repaired in order to prevent invasions by the Mongolians. If the Spanish Empire had aligned themselves with such forces, such an alliance may well have increased their chances of mounting a successful invasion of China.

What if...

THE RAF HAD LOST THE BATTLE OF BRITAIN?

The possible consequences of Britain's aerial defeat in 1940 have fascinated historians and perplexed military strategists for decades

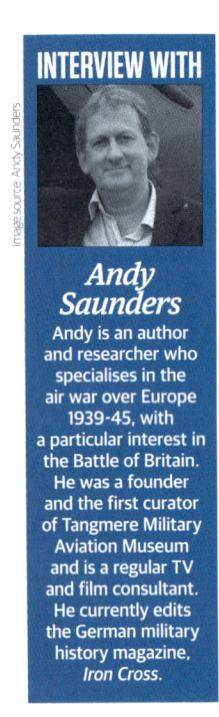

INTERVIEW WITH

Andy Saunders

Andy is an author and researcher who specialises in the air war over Europe 1939-45, with a particular interest in the Battle of Britain. He was a founder and the first curator of Tangmere Military Aviation Museum and is a regular TV and film consultant. He currently edits the German military history magazine, *Iron Cross*.

RIGHT Photograph taken from within a German bomber showing a Spitfire hit by enemy fire

The Battle of Britain was a critical moment in World War II, a tussle that saw the Royal Air Force and other British services stop the German Luftwaffe gaining air superiority over the UK. Since the end of the war many historians have speculated and debated the possible outcomes if the RAF had been defeated in 1940. This usually centres on the idea that a defeat would have been followed by the Nazi invasion of Britain. Operation Sea Lion, as the German invasion plan was called, could have ultimately led to the complete and irremediable defeat of Britain and her vast empire.

However, while the defeat of the RAF might not necessarily have led to invasion (and if it had, such an invasion attempt might well have failed) it would have certainly set in motion a very different series of events for the remainder of the war.

Why was the Battle of Britain such a critical moment for Britain and Nazi Germany?

By the early summer of 1940 Germany had defeated and occupied the majority of Western Europe, while Britain had suffered the ignominious military disaster of defeat in France, Belgium and Norway. Nevertheless, Britain, its empire and the free Allies still stood between Germany and the complete control and domination it desired. To achieve that goal, Germany needed to eliminate Britain as an effective fighting power. Whether it did that through military invasion, or subjugation by other means, was almost an irrelevance. What mattered, if it was to achieve any such aim, was to gain total air superiority. In other words, to defeat the RAF – and, specifically, RAF Fighter Command.

While it might be stretching a point to say that only the RAF stood between invasion and defeat, it was nevertheless a fact that the elimination of the RAF as an effective fighting force was essential if Germany wanted to beat Britain – whether that be by achieving the air superiority necessary for invasion or through bombing Britain into submission through uncontested air attacks.

What was the main reason the RAF was able to stop the Nazis gaining air superiority in 1940?

The most crucial element was the RAF's integrated command and control system. Known colloquially as 'The Dowding System' (after the commander-in-chief of RAF Fighter Command) it incorporated an early warning system through radar and the Observer Corps, allowing commanders to marshal their fighters in a timely fashion and appropriate numbers, and by placing them in the most advantageous tactical position: up-sun, at a higher altitude and aiming to cut off the enemy's approach to target. It did not always work perfectly, but it did allow the RAF's controllers to manage the battle and it thus gave the defenders a great advantage.

What might the Luftwaffe have done differently in the summer of 1940 to defeat the RAF?

Had the Luftwaffe stuck rigidly to its

What if...
THE RAF HAD LOST THE BATTLE OF BRITAIN?

What if... THE RAF HAD LOST THE BATTLE OF BRITAIN?

THE PAST

1940
RAF VICTORY
By the autumn of 1940 the Luftwaffe campaign against the RAF was beginning to weaken. On 17 September Hitler suspended Operation Sea Lion – the planned invasion of the UK – and 31 October saw the final daylight raid by the Luftwaffe. Although seriously weakened, the RAF had successfully stopped the Germans gaining air superiority over Britain.

1940-41
THE BLITZ
After it was realised the Luftwaffe had failed to gain air superiority over the UK, the Nazis switched to a focus on nighttime bombing raids. Known simply as the Blitz, for several months German bombers targeted major cities and industrial centres, but also the civilian population. Despite the widespread devastation and loss of life, the British morale remained strong, and the 'Blitz Spirit' of defiant endurance was used in propaganda efforts to maintain support for the war effort.

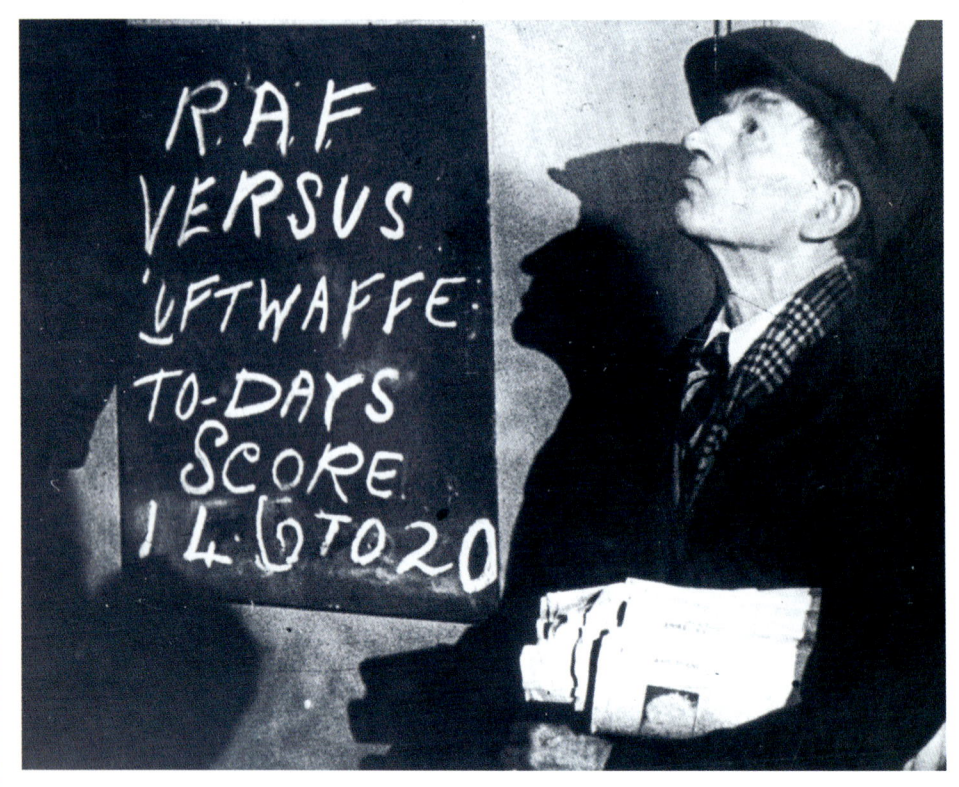

1942
"REAP THE WHIRLWIND"
Continuing its offensive operations begun during the Battle of Britain, the RAF expanded greatly in the aftermath of 1940 and developed more-effective tactics and technologies to take the fight back to Nazi Germany. In 1942 Arthur 'Bomber' Harris was made Air Marshal of Bomber Command, and began a campaign of strategic area bombing against Germany, stating: "They sowed the wind, and now they are going to reap the whirlwind." One of the first major bombing operations was on the night of 30 May, during which over 1,000 RAF aircraft bombed the city of Cologne, destroying approximately 13,000 buildings.

---

attacks on RAF airfields (particularly fighter bases), and to infrastructure such as the radar stations, then it would have had a much better chance of bringing Fighter Command to its knees. When it moved away from those targets in late August it did so just at a point when the raids were starting to tell. A relentless continuation and focus on those targets would have finally borne fruit.

Shifting the bombing to cities, industrial targets and ports etc, including night bombing raids, was a grave tactical error by the Nazis because the Luftwaffe really needed to knock out the RAF's defensive capability.

ABOVE
A newspaper seller next to a board with the latest 'score' of the Battle of Britain

BELOW
London's St Paul's Cathedral seen through the smoke after a night of Luftwaffe bombing

If the Luftwaffe had won, would daytime bombing have increased? And what capacity did the Germans have to increase bombing raids?
If the Luftwaffe had been victorious in defeating RAF Fighter Command, then it would have been able to increase daylight bombing operations and range across Britain at will and relatively unhindered, and it would have had capacity to do so. Daylight bombing was far more accurate than bombing by night – as in the Blitz. It would have enabled concentrated targeting to bring about the destruction of infrastructure, warehousing, docks, communications, manufacturing, remaining military targets, food supplies and more. In this manner, Germany might have theoretically secured the defeat of Britain and its neutralisation as a fighting power without any need for a risky cross-Channel invasion.

What impact might an increase in bombing have had on Britain's war effort and morale?
An increase in bombing (in the event of RAF Fighter Command defeat) might have been catastrophic for Britain's continuation with the war if its ability to manufacture or import was sufficiently depleted. However, in such an eventuality as the defeat of the RAF, there would have been no purpose in the Luftwaffe 'terror bombing' the civilian population. The effort would have been militarily and tactically wasted, although public morale

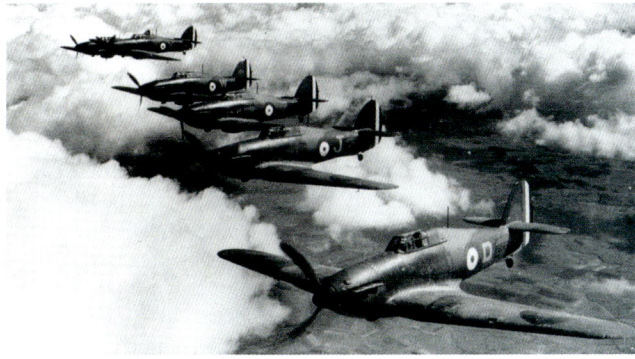

delight in, "knowing the worst." He also judged that to the British, "the possibility of defeat is neither imagined, nor imaginable." This, of course, was when Dunkirk had been perceived as 'victorious', the Battle of Britain had been won and the population buoyed-up by the rhetoric of Winston Churchill. All of that may have changed if the British population was truly staring defeat in the face.

If the RAF had been defeated, was a German invasion or a British surrender more likely?

Even with air superiority wrested from the RAF, it was not a given that invasion would have followed because such an operation was fraught with danger and difficulty - even with Fighter Command out of the way. Part of the problem for Germany was the logistical issue of getting an invasion force across the Channel because it simply did not have either the right vessels or sufficient numbers of them.

Additionally, the Luftwaffe had lost a huge percentage of its Ju 52 transport fleet in Holland and many key naval vessels in Norway, and with the Royal Navy still immensely powerful its Home Fleet would have impeded invasion attempts. However, the Royal Navy's ships would have been very vulnerable to Luftwaffe attack (particularly from the Ju 87 Stuka) without fighter cover from the RAF. Also, and again without fighter cover, Bomber Command would have intervened.

The occupying force would also need to be fed and supplied, and supply lines may have been challenging.

Was it possible the RAF could have been rebuilt to defend Britain?

Had RAF Fighter Command been defeated, and no invasion or occupation of Britain had subsequently occurred, then it might theoretically have been possible to rebuild the fighter force. However, this would have been contingent upon the ability to continue aircraft production in undamaged factories (there was never a shortage of aircraft, only of pilots) or potentially the import of suitable American fighters - although this would all have taken time.

The rebuilding of RAF capability within Britain would also have been reliant upon the supply of raw materials, that the Luftwaffe did not then focus on the destruction of aircraft factories, and that enough pilots could be trained and made operational in good time.

may have begun to buckle if it saw or realised that its erstwhile saviours, the RAF, had already been defeated.

That said, the Ministry of Information's Home Security Unit monitored morale in the Blitz, and while the reaction of civilians was variable it was over-arched by grumbles and grievances rather than any doom-laden crumbling of morale. One of the leaders of the organisation monitoring morale wrote: "The British are pragmatic and with a stability of temperament, albeit with a slightly gloomy tinge."

He went on to say that they tended towards self-righteous indignation when things went wrong and had a masochistic

ABOVE-TOP
A British soldier guarding a German Messerschmitt Bf 109 fighter plane, which had been intercepted over the English Channel and shot down

ABOVE-MIDDLE
Hawker Hurricanes in formation during 1940

ABOVE
Messerschmitt Bf110 bombers in formation flight

THE POSSIBILITY

1940

LUFTWAFFE SUPERIORITY
With RAF Fighter Command crippled or destroyed, the Luftwaffe would have reigned supreme in British airspace. With no fighter aircraft to pose any threat, Luftwaffe bombers could launch a greater number of bombing raids on Britain's industrial centres and major cities. The benefit of bombing during the daytime would have made these raids far more accurate and therefore devastating for Britain's war industry.

1941

BLITZ SPIRIT BROKEN
In a speech to Parliament after the evacuation of Dunkirk, Winston Churchill was able to rally the morale of the public by drawing great confidence from the RAF's successes against the Luftwaffe. The defeat of the RAF during the summer of 1940 would therefore have come as a shock to many, and certainly a dark moment during a war that so far had seen few if any significant victories for the Allies. The unrestricted bombing of British factories and cities would have had a further impact on public morale, as well as Britain's war industry. Though an invasion of the mainland UK may still not have taken place, Britain's factories and port towns would have been heavily damaged during the bombings, greatly reducing Britain's ability to continue the war.

What if...

JOAN OF ARC HADN'T BROKEN THE SIEGE OF ORLEANS?

A teenage girl in armour, with a God-given vision of victory, held the fate of France in her hands

INTERVIEW WITH

Sharon Bennett Connolly

Sharon is a fellow of the Royal Historical Society and best-selling author of *Heroines of the Medieval World*, *Silk and the Sword: The Women of the Norman Conquest*, and *Ladies of Magna Carta: Women of Influence in Thirteenth Century England*. Her fourth book, *Defenders of the Norman Crown: Rise and Fall of the Warenne Earls of Surrey*, was released in May 2021. She also writes the popular history blog, www.historythe interestingbits.com.

The Hundred Years' War (1337 – 1453) raged on between England and France, with its complex and cutthroat world of royal claim and counterclaim over titles and land. Through all the manoeuvring of armies and political games of princes came a young woman with a message of simple faith and passion for her country. Her words would be an inspiration to all around her, and her courage would give real hope to all who wanted to free France from the grip of the English throne. The Siege of Orleans in 1429 would prove a pivotal moment to believe in, or doubt, Joan of Arc, and for the very future of France itself.

How strategically important was the siege and how may the war have been altered if it had not been broken by Joan of Arc?
Orleans was important for both France and for Joan of Arc. For Joan it was a test to prove that she could deliver on what she had promised. For France, it was the start of the fight back against the English occupation. Another victory at Patay in June 1429 saw the English routed; their reputation for invincibility was destroyed with the French achieving an impressive victory. The road was open for Joan's troops to advance on Paris and preparations could be made for the dauphin's coronation at Reims. It all started with Orleans.

A city that had been besieged for six months was freed in four days. Joan's lightning success established her credentials and her reputation. Had she failed at Orleans her career would have been short-lived indeed, and she may well have paid with her life. Having persuaded the dauphin to have faith in her, her failure would've been an embarrassment to him and he could have easily ordered her execution.

What unique qualities did Joan have, or what exceptional circumstances prevailed, which meant she could succeed where others had failed?
Joan had an inherent belief in her destiny and duty. In her early teens she began to experience visions and heard the voices of St Michael the Archangel, St Catherine of Alexandria and St Margaret of Antioch. While we are largely dismissive of such claims in the 21st century, in the early 15th century it was not unknown for maids to claim to be guided by saints and be believed. In a less scientific world, such events were received with far less cynicism. In May 1428, guided by her voices, Joan travelled to Vaucouleurs, the nearest garrison loyal to France and the dauphin, and asked the garrison commander, Robert de Baudricourt, for permission to join the dauphin. By January 1429, she had gained the respect of the people through her quiet firmness and piety, and she finally managed to persuade Baudricourt that she was neither a witch nor feebleminded. Charles was not the most pro-active of military leaders and it took the arrival of Joan of Arc to spur him into some sort of action. Joan was supremely confident in her position at the French court. Just two months after arriving, she wrote to the duke of Bedford, the English regent in France, ordering him to "hand over to the Maiden, who is sent by God the King of Heaven, the keys to

RIGHT The Siege of Orleans would define Joan's success and her eventual fate

What if…
JOAN OF ARC HADN'T BROKEN THE SIEGE OF ORLEANS?

The Daily Gazette

YOUTH JAILED
Joan of Arc arrested for heresy

What if... JOAN OF ARC HADN'T BROKEN THE SIEGE OF ORLEANS?

THE PAST

1425
VISIONS OF HOPE
At around the age of 12 or 13 Joan claimed to have first heard three voices of 'angels'. At first, they encouraged her to be pious, obedient and live a good Christian life, very much in the manner of her deeply religious mother. But as time went by the message changed. Now the voices, and in some cases visions, of the angels instructed Joan to rid France of its enemy the English, and to make sure the dauphin Charles was crowned king at Reims. Convinced she had been chosen by God for the task, Joan set out to accomplish her goal.

1429
KING MAKER
Despite a mix of scepticism and outright disbelief at Joan's claims, she used her unwavering faith and self-belief to persuade enough influential people to get an audience with the dauphin, Charles, heir to the throne of France. Charles in turn was not completely convinced by her, and had his ecclesiastical advisors question her extensively. It would seem, however, that he was willing to take a chance. Joan fulfilled her promise to lift the Siege of Orleans and also played a significant role in the crowning of the new King Charles VII at Reims, as she had predicted.

1431
MARTYR TO THE CAUSE
Joan's brief yet intense military career was not all plain sailing. She failed to take Paris but did succeed in liberating several towns from the English. But it was her capture by forces of the duke of Burgundy that was to lead to her downfall. Eventually put on ecclesiastical trial for heresy, the strength of her defence when questioned forced the proceedings be moved from public view into private session to save embarrassment for her inquisitors. Many charges were dropped, but ironically it was the heretical act of dressing like a man that stuck, resulting in Joan being sentenced to death and burnt at the stake.

all the towns which you have taken and violated in France. She has come here in the name of God to support the Royal Family [of France]. She is quite prepared to make peace, if you are willing to do right so long as you give up France and make amends for occupying it." That's an impressive amount of confidence for a teenage peasant!

How do you think she would have reacted if she'd failed to break the Siege of Orleans? What action would she have taken?
I don't think Joan would have seen failure as a possibility. She broke the siege in four days. It is possible that she could have taken longer, and that she may have needed reinforcements, but she had staked everything on taking Orleans – failure was not an option. The siege was broken by systematically taking the forts that the English had erected to encircle the city. If the French had not been able to do this, then other tactics could've been used, such as besieging the besiegers. The battle would've lasted longer and expended men and supplies, and would not have cemented Joan's reputation in quite the same way as breaking the siege in just four days did.

What was Joan's possible fate had she not broken the siege?
Had she not broken the siege, I am not sure she would have been given a second chance. She had told her interrogators at Poitiers that she would prove herself at Orleans – it was make or break for her. In medieval times, men were even more reluctant than nowadays to take orders from a woman – let alone an uneducated teenage peasant girl. The best she could have hoped for was to be sent home with an instruction to 'never come back'. The more likely outcome would have been execution for embarrassing the dauphin and the leaders of the French royal court.

BELOW-LEFT
Some nobles were unhappy with Joan's role in the coronation of Charles VII

BELOW-RIGHT
Joan was strong and defiant at her trial

How weakened would the French Church and Crown have been without Joan as a rallying point in the war?
I'm not sure France could have been weakened any more than it already was. Joan appeared at one of the lowest points in French history. At the time of her birth, France had endured years of intermittent warfare with successive English kings since Edward III had attempted to assert their claims to its crown. Civil war between the Armagnac and Burgundian factions at the French court had practically paralysed the country at the turn of the century, making her susceptible to renewed English aggression. Far from being a united country, a great part of France was made up of semi-independent duchies, such as Burgundy and Brittany, whose rulers often sided with the English against their French overlord. In the early 1400s France was ruled by Charles VI, a king with such mental problems that, at times, he thought that he was made of glass. English 'diplomacy' following their great victory at the Battle of Agincourt in October 1415 had persuaded Charles VI to disinherit his own son, the Dauphin Charles, and name Henry V of England as his heir. With Charles not being the most pro-active of military leaders, it is hard to see where a breakthrough could have been made had Joan of Arc not come along.

Was Joan truly a major influence on events and decisions, or just a puppet of the major players in the war?
The triumphs of Joan of Arc were remarkable due not only to the fact she was a simple country girl, but also because she was a teenager – and a girl! The king of France considered her contribution to be significant and remarkable. In the last days of December 1429, he issued letters patent ennobling Joan, her parents and her brothers. She was a peasant no longer, and her whole family was given recognition

ABOVE
A young Henry VI of England was crowned king of France but was never recognised by the French

for the contribution Joan had made to getting Charles crowned and to France's extraordinary recovery. She'd done what no one else in France had been able to do: she had led the fight back against the English and given France and its king back their dignity. And yet she was still a pawn for powerful men in the greater conflict; the English saw her destruction as essential to victory over the French and Charles VII would not lift a finger to help her for fear it would jeopardise the brokering of peace with the duke of Burgundy.

How significant to subsequent events were Joan's trial and execution by the English and inevitable martyrdom by the French?
Joan's trial and execution was a political necessity if the English were ever to regain the upper hand in the war against France. Or, maybe, it was a sign of English desperation? They knew they were losing and were not going down without a fight. Joan's death did not change the outcome of the war when all is said and done. An inquiry into her trial, in 1456, heard from those present at her execution, who said that they didn't doubt her salvation and that she died a faithful Christian. The inquiry had been ordered by Pope Callixtus III following appeals from Joan's family. Charles VII had conducted an initial inquiry in 1450 but the pope's hearings went further, revoking and annulling the 1431 sentence; Joan was innocent. However, she would not be canonised until the 20th century – on 16 May 1920 Pope Benedict XV declared her a saint with her feast day on 30 May, the date of her death. Joan of Arc is the epitome of the medieval heroine. It is incredible to think what she achieved at such an early age, in so short a time; her story takes up less than three years of French history and yet it resonates through the ages. Her military career lasted just 18 months but, in that time, she took numerous towns and cities, her greatest achievement being the relief of Orleans, which secured the loyalty of much of northern France to the French crown. She revitalised the French army and people, saw her king crowned, almost took Paris, and put France on the road that would eventually see it victorious in the Hundred Years' War. With no formal military training she led armies into battle at 17. With no education, she advised her king on policy and military tactics, and managed to hold her own against the greatest theologians her enemies could bring against her.

THE POSSIBILITY

1429

FROM DAUPHIN TO NOTHING
It could be argued that, with all his dithering in the face of the English threat, without the passionate drive of Joan of Arc the future Charles VII may never have become king at all. Her belief in divine intervention was the driving force behind his coronation, having safely escorted him through enemy territory to make it happen just the way she'd been told by the angels. A weak dauphin, without Joan's success at Orleans to prove God was on his side, would have been an easy target for the English to cement their claim to the throne.

1444

A VERY DIFFERENT DYNASTY
A truce between the English and French caused rejoicing on both sides, but a marriage between Henry VI and Margaret of Anjou – a niece of Charles VII by marriage – could seal the deal. But if Orleans had not fallen, and the war had gone the way of the English, such a marriage may not have been necessary. If Henry had married someone else, then the possibilities of his heirs creating an altogether different dynastic path in history is possible. If so, then there may have been no Wars of the Roses, no Richard III, and even no Tudors!

1453 ONWARDS

UNITED KINGDOM OF ENGLAND AND FRANCE
With the claim of Charles VII not successful, the English with the upper hand, and an English king of both England and France, there would have been far more possibilities for a firm English grip on France, both in land and power, rather than the fractured pieces of territory and shallow title future monarchs would inherit. Their joint resources would have proved troublesome for other powers in Europe, particularly Spain, giving the English throne far greater influence far sooner than was the case in reality.

What if...

SOUTH AMERICA HAD JOINED WORLD WAR I?

If Britain had convinced Chile and Argentina to side with the Allies, the Great War could have been a truly global conflict

INTERVIEW WITH

Dr Phillip Dehne

Professor of history at St John's College, New York, Dr Philip Dehne is the author of *On the Far Western Front: Britain's First World War in South America*. He has also penned several articles related to the economic conflict during World War I.

What was Latin America's mentality towards Europe during World War I?
That would depend on where you were. Mexico was tilted into the conflict as a result of its proximity to the US, and because of things like the Zimmermann telegram [an intercepted communication from Germany proposing an alliance with Mexico]. Some people in Latin America were really stirred by the conflict. Certain ethnic communities, and the British and Germans, immediately jumped on boats and came back to Europe to join the forces.

People were freaked out by the war when it started but in August and September of 1914, the Latin American general public was really intrigued by the news of what was going on because so many of them were immigrants – particularly Italians and a fair number of British people. There were lots of people who still identified with Europe in cities like Buenos Aires. So many of those living there were immigrants or their children. It was an immediate thing, even though they were thousands of miles away.

Antarctic explorer Ernest Shackleton was sent as a British envoy to persuade Argentina and Chile to join the Allies in 1917. Why was he unsuccessful?
There were desires of the British to get the Argentines involved and there were some ways that they could induce them. They would have been allowed to more or less take control of German ships in their harbours and they could have done things like take control of German businesses.

But the Allied cause wasn't popular enough – especially the British cause. It wasn't particularly favoured among the general public in Argentina and definitely not among the political leaders during the war. Being anti-British was pretty popular.

I believe they wouldn't join the war because the inducements were not enough. Shackleton's visit was big news when it happened and there were later efforts too, like the high-level British diplomatic De Bunsen Mission in 1918.

The Argentine leaders, like President [Hipólito] Yrigoyen, didn't see enough benefit in joining. Remaining neutral was a great way for Latin American politicians to prove to their public that they were truly looking out for them – they were putting Argentina before British businesses and imperial governments. They could have taken control of German business and there were potential benefits but it would have been a political problem to come down on the side of the Allies.

Yrigoyen was seen as being in the pocket of the Americans and he was trying to change that.

Was there anything that could have convinced them?
Well, I imagine that there were all sorts of rumours going around that members of his government could be bought and then the story the British often told where some members of his administration were probably being bought off by the Germans in order to push this neutralist stance. So I don't know that there would have been a possibility of bribing their way through the policy.

Maybe they could have been more open, there could have been some sort of loan given to the Argentines, although they didn't really need any sort of loan at the time. They could have been given inducements like large amounts of coal

RIGHT
Antarctic explorer Ernest Shackleton was sent as a British envoy to persuade Argentina and Chile to join the Allies in 1917

What if...
SOUTH AMERICA HAD JOINED WORLD WAR I?

"There were lots of people who identified with Europe in cities"

What if... SOUTH AMERICA HAD JOINED WORLD WAR I?

– they certainly needed that for their railways. But the Allies basically got what they wanted out of Argentina during the war anyway. They were still getting as much food as they wanted.

So did Argentina kind of support the Allies anyway?
Yes, just by its willingness to sell. Of course, it had to sell to someone but it was willing to sell food to the Allies in 1917 and 1918. Half of the meat consumed by Allied soldiers came from Argentina, along with huge amounts of wheat and other grains. Some historians argue that these were really deals that benefited the Allies more than Argentina but I disagree – I think these deals really served Argentina, too.

It would have been sort of intriguing if they had joined the war. Maybe there would have been more domestic crackdown because of the Germans in Argentina. It's easy to imagine them crushing the German community more definitively.

Was Germany trying to get Argentina and Chile on board with its own war effort?
Germany's main goal in South America was to keep the nations there neutral – there was no attempt like the Zimmermann telegram. They were very keen on keeping their connections with South America, and Germany had had a really significant role in the Chilean military and a variety of other armies in South America before the war, so they had long-term diplomatic and commercial ties for quite a while. The Germans certainly hoped to keep those open post-war and they were quite successful.

If Argentina and Chile had entered the war, what would have been different?
I guess the long-term changes would have been to the German communities and Germany's connection with Latin America. The latter probably would have been the biggest change if Chile and Argentina had declared their allegiance to the Allies. The way the war was fought, there probably wouldn't have been Chilean or Argentinian soldiers or navies floating on the seas. Brazil did join the war [in 1917] and there weren't really any significant military benefits from them joining.

Would it have changed Argentina's global standing?
It would have indicated a much closer relationship with the US than they ended up having – their ties were kind of touchy throughout the post-war years. Argentina actually had a really interesting position in post-war global politics. Because it stood up and refused to join the war, it was considered unique and led the group of neutrals, which could be seen in its work in the League of Nations. Had they joined the war, it would have been possible that Argentina and Great Britain would have had a very different relationship throughout much of the 20th century. The Falklands War in the 1980s was a bit of an apotheosis of the problems between the countries. If they became closer, there was the possibility for some sort of transatlantic relationship for Britain, beyond the one with the US.

What about Chile's standing after World War I?
Chile made a lot of money in the nitrates trade during the war, which was very important for explosives, but that collapsed with peace and the creation of technological innovations that put nitrates out of business. In many ways, Chile had a similar wariness of European imperialism to the Argentines.

The short-term benefits of Chile joining the war would have been the same as Argentina – they could have commandeered German ships in their harbours and taken over German businesses in their country if they had wanted to. Then they could have created a longer-term transatlantic

HOW WOULD IT BE DIFFERENT?

REAL TIMELINE

28 July 1914 – World War I
Austria declares war on Serbia, sparking the conflict in Europe and leading to further declarations of war from other nations.

5 April 1917 – Brazil enters WWI
One of Brazil's steamships is torpedoed by a German submarine, ultimately leading to Brazil declaring war on Germany.

October 1917 – Shackleton sets sail
British explorer Ernest Shackleton heads to South America to try and get Argentina and Chile to join the Allies.

ALTERNATE TIMELINE

April 1918 – Shackleton unsuccessful
With few incentives to offer them, the explorer's diplomatic mission fails. Chile and Argentina remain neutral parties in the war.

April 1918 – A new alliance
Promising them British coal as well as the right to seize German ships and businesses, Shackleton convinces Chile and Argentina to fight

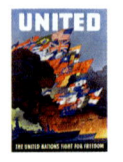

ABOVE
The 1914 Battle of Coronel saw the Imperial German Navy defeat the Royal Navy off the coast of Chile, could it have been different with regional support?

relationship with the British or the US. But there were no strategic benefits to either of them [for entering the war] – there was no German land they could grab.

If Chile had entered the war, would things have been different there?
I guess one of the more apocalyptic scenarios was that if the Chilean government had joined the war, the half a million Germans living there would have risen up out of anger. On the other hand, a lot of the Germans were there because they didn't really want to live in their homeland any more. Some of them were just happy to be immigrants.

How would Chile's relationship with the US have been different after the war if they had entered?
I guess it would have been similar to what could have happened with Argentina. The US swooped in pretty quickly after the Germans were pushed out by the blockade and the British were focusing on other markets. America was already moving in during the war, so historians think Chile was more worried by the American incursions into their markets than the Argentines were. Chile seemed so far away for the US. You would have been hard pressed to find anyone in the US who cared if Chile joined the war or not.

Did Brazil entering the war in 1917 – the only Latin American country to do so – play a part in Argentina not joining?
What Brazil got out of joining the war was a bit of status. They wanted to show they would support the US, that it was a hemisphere solidarity. The Brazilians and Argentines really didn't get along with one another at all, so it's not at all surprising that Brazil joined the war and then Argentina refused to. What the Brazilians got out of the war was proof for themselves and for other countries that they were an important government.

After the war, the Brazilians were invited to the Paris Peace Conference, so they brought a delegation. They didn't play a significant role but they were trying to talk of themselves as being a real world power. At the conference, for instance, there was talk about giving Brazil a permanent seat on the council of the League of Nations, which was being created.

The Brazilian-Argentine dynamic was always a rocky one but the Brazilians felt they got more or less what they wanted from the war. They got some prestige from it, and were welcome at the big table when it came to creating the post-war world.

What did this do for relations between Brazil and Argentina?
You could find Argentine publications that sneered at the Brazilians for joining the war. But then again you could find some Argentines smearing their government for not joining the war. When you bring Brazil into it, it highlights the enormity of the rivalry between the two countries. It would have been hard to imagine them both doing the same thing during the conflict, especially because there was no German threat to either of them.

What effect did World War I have on Latin America?
World War I played a gigantic role in the development of these nations. As a result of the conflict, they became increasingly against globalisation and more nationalistic in their economic and political outlooks. In that way it was a turning point in the history of Latin America in general.

Whether or not these countries entered the war, the war entered their lives – it really impacted them tremendously. Latin America was not alone in the 1920s and 1930s of striving against economic globalisation and I think that, in some ways, their wariness of the rest of the world has been a defining characteristic of Latin American relations with the rest of the world ever since.

July 1918
German army collapses
After gaining ground via the Spring Offensives, the German Army crumbles in the face of intense resistance.

January 1919
Paris Peace Conference
The Allied powers meet to set the peace terms for the defeated nations, with Brazil playing its part proudly.

June 1919
Treaty of Versailles
Harsh terms are laid on Germany for its part in the war, sending the country into economic turmoil.

1982
Falklands War
Increasing tension between Argentina and Britain leads to a conflict over the sovereignty of the Falkland Islands.

May 1918
Supplies flow
Argentina and Chile increase their flow of supplies to Britain and the Allies, significantly helping the war effort.

November 1918
Armistice Day
On the brink of defeat, Germany signs an armistice with the Allies, bringing World War I to an end.

1919
American relations
Chile strikes up a strong trade agreement with the US as the country celebrates its higher standing in the world.

1982
Falklands Peace
Argentina and Britain find common ground over the Falklands conflict without needing to resort to violence.

June 1918
Kaiser forces pushed back
With renewed support, the Allies are able to bring the German army to its knees sooner.

October 1918
Early victory
The Germans sign an armistice with the Allies, with Argentina and Chile playing their part in the victory.

December 1918
Global players
Both Argentina and Chile send delegations to the conference to take part in the peace conference, embracing globalisation.

1920
British relations
Relations between Argentina and Britain flourish and anti-British sentiment begins to fade in Latin America.

What if...

BOUDICCA'S REVOLUTION HAD SUCCEEDED?

In 60-61 CE the queen of the Iceni tribe led a bloody rebellion that very nearly ended the Roman occupation of Britain

INTERVIEW WITH

Dr Simon Elliott

Dr Elliott is a bestselling author, historian, archaeologist and broadcaster, with books such as *Roman Conquests: Britain*. In June 2022 he led his week-long tour 'Boudicca: Heroic Queen of Britannia' for Hidden History Travel.

At the time of Boudicca, the Roman occupation of 'Britannia' was relatively new, but there was already a form of peace and mutual acceptance, even co-existence, with many of the native tribes, the Iceni included. But the tiger will always use its claws, and the opportunity for Rome to increase its wealth, territory and power after the death of Iceni king Prasutagus in c.60-61 CE was too good to miss. The resulting violence and dishonouring of the Iceni sparked a revolt against the Romans that would settle the balance of power in Britannia for centuries to come.

How were the Boudiccan rebels able to initially defeat the Romans in the revolt the queen led in c.60-61 CE?
At the heart of this answer is the specific time when the Boudiccan Revolt broke out. This was effectively the halfway point in the Roman campaigns of conquests in Britain in the 1st century CE. This had begun with the Claudian invasion in 43 CE under Aulus Plautius which, by the end of that year, had established the capital of the new province in modern Colchester. (Previously Camulodunum, capital of the native British Catuvellauni.) It ended with Agricola's final campaign around 83 CE when he defeated the Caledonians at the Battle of Mons Graupius in the Grampians, and then ordered the Classis Britannica regional fleet to circumnavigate the main island of Britain. As each stage of conquest moved forward step by step from southeast to northwest, the Romans set up a series of 'stop lines' to allow them to plan their next advance.

Once ready, a new campaign then began. This is what was happening in the period immediately prior to the Boudiccan Revolt when, after a pause, the governor Gaius Suetonius Paulinus began a new campaign to subjugate the northwest of Wales. His eye was off the ball to his rear when, after the death of their client king Prasutagus, Roman mistreatment of his Iceni tribe in north Norfolk led to Prasutagus' widow Boudicca leading her revolt. The Romans were caught cold because their legions were deployed so far away: legio XIV Gemina and legio XX Valeria Victrix were with Paulinus, legio II Augusta was in Exeter, and legio IX Hispana in was southern Lincolnshire. In short, the Romans completely overplayed their hand in terms of civil government when trying to incorporate the territory of the Iceni into the province, and when things went badly for them they didn't have the available military resources to deal with the fall out.

How was Boudicca able to rally support for her cause?
Historians, ancient and modern, have often focused on the Iceni response to their disastrous rift with the Romans, but we should remember this was a new province, with the tribes of the south east subjugated longest. The nobility of the Trinovantes in southern modern Essex,

RIGHT
Governor Paulinus eventually defeated Boudicca and saved Rome's reputation

What if...
BOUDICCA'S REVOLUTION HAD SUCCEEDED?

What if... BOUDICCA'S REVOLUTION HAD SUCCEEDED?

THE PAST

C.60-61 CE

THE DEATH OF PRASUTAGUS

Even though he may have had good intentions, what the Iceni King Prasutagus actually left as his legacy was the spark that ignited a bloody revolt. By leaving his kingdom equally between his daughters and the Emperor Nero (pictured), the Iceni leader wished for his reign to live on through his offspring and for the co-existence with the Romans to continue. But Prasutagus' faith in the future and in the Romans was dreadfully misplaced, and the emperor and his governor in Britannia had other ideas.

C.60-61 CE

ROME SNATCHES IT ALL

Not surprisingly, rather than comply with the wishes of the dead Iceni king, Rome decided to flex its considerable muscles and show who was boss. Simply ignoring the Iceni king's legacy, the Roman governor Paulinus annexed his lands and humiliated his people, (including his widow and daughters) through slaughter, torture and abuse. No thought or regard was given for any kind of fragile agreements or treaties. It was a reality check for the tribes of Britannia – Rome could just about do whatever it wanted.

C.60-61 CE

A QUEEN FIGHTS FOR HER HONOUR

The Iceni Queen Boudicca was incensed by the brutality of the Romans and their lack of honour towards her, her family and her people, and she rallied support among the Iceni and other tribes to rise up against the Romans. An army of tens of thousands plundered and destroyed Camulodunum (Colchester), then Londinium (London) and finally Verulamium (St Albans). As many as 80,000 Britons and Romans may have been killed in the fighting. The Roman governor Paulinius finally defeated Boudicca in what is known as the Battle of Watling Street (61 CE). Legend has it she poisoned herself rather than be captured, but her fate is unknown.

ABOVE Boudicca inspired her people to rise up against Roman rule

RIGHT Defeat would have made Emperor Nero's position even more fragile

---

the Catuvellauni to the west through to modern Hertfordshire, the Atrebates in the Thames Valley and the Cantiaci in Kent had all adopted Roman ways. They sponsored stone public buildings for the first time, sent their sons to Rome to be educated and wore togas when carrying out the new responsibilities of Roman civil government. All of this required funding in the form of loans to the aristocracy from the wealthy in Rome. This was burdensome for the leading Britons, and it seems as soon as a realistic opportunity presented itself to throw off the yoke of Rome the leading regional aristocrats did so, aligning their fate to that of Boudicca and the Iceni. The interesting question here is why did the Cantiaci not join the revolt? The answer is perhaps because they were at that time the most Romanised of the British tribes given their proximity to the continent.

If success against the Romans had continued would other tribes have joined in the revolt?
This is a very interesting question. I think we can be sure the Trinovantes, Catuvellauni and most likely the Atrebates joined the Iceni, but did others? Certainly, when Paulinus began his forced march from Wales towards the southeast he was building marching camps for his troops at the end of each day's march. This indicates that although once into the Welsh Marches he was back in his province, he felt he was now in enemy territory once more given the conflagration taking place in East Anglia. At the very least this shows a distrust of the 'conquered' tribal confederations there, for example the Dobunni and Coritani. I believe these and others would then have joined the rebellion if the Romans had lost their decisive engagement with Boudicca after the sack of St Albans. That, of course, would be dependent on any Romans being left to rebel against after such a catastrophe.

How would a Roman defeat have changed the political and social makeup of Britain in the future?
Roman Britain was always the wild northwest of the empire. It was a place of difference because the far north was never fully conquered, and it required a huge military presence to maintain the northern border. I estimate that around 12% of the entire military establishment was in only 4% of the geographic area of the empire. If you add to this Britain's distance from Rome, and the fact it was separated from the continent by the terrifying Oceanus, as the Romans knew the English Channel and North Sea, then you have one of the most marginal provinces in the empire. On a number of occasions I think Roman emperors considered abandoning their occupation here, one certainly in the context of the Boudiccan Revolt when Nero must surely have wondered if the province was worth the effort of holding. To that end, if Paulinus had lost his decisive engagement I think that the Romans would have abandoned Britain, perhaps never to return. It is no coincidence that when Paulinus' order for Legio II Augusta to join him in the Midlands reached its stand in-commander Poenius Postumus in Exeter, he refused to move. The reason? Just to the south was

the port of the legionary fortress, a fine harbour located at modern Topsham on the River Exe. The praefectus castrorum was making sure that he and his men could escape back to the continent if, as he expected, the governor was defeated.

Any Roman abandonment of Britain, especially in such shocking circumstances, would have had profound implications for later British history. It is very likely, given the youth of the province at this point, that the various tribal regions would have reasserted their territorial identities, including the reestablishment of their original borders. Internecine warfare would then have followed as each struggled for regional dominance, with perhaps Boudicca for a time being the most influential figure across the main island of Britain. Furthermore, given some have speculated Boudicca was actually born on the continent (for example among the Batavi in the Rhine Delta), an eventual victory for her in Britain may also have impacted the narrative of Roman dominance in the continental west.

With a united Britain would future invasions (for example by the Germans in the 4th and 5th centuries CE, and later the Vikings) have been less successful?
I don't think there was any chance at all that the native Britons would have united under one leader in the long term in the wake of a Roman withdrawal. Much more likely, as I set out previously, would have been a return to the pre-Roman tribal identities, loyalties and borders. In short, normal service would have resumed.

What would defeat to Boudicca have meant to the reputation of the Roman Empire and Nero?
The emperor, the Roman political establishment and the Roman military all knew that the Boudiccan Revolt was a close run thing. They all knew that the great Emperor Augustus' lowest moment had been the loss of Varus' three legions to the Germans in the Teutoburg Forest in 9 CE, and the jeopardy in Britain in 60/61 CE was even greater, with four legions in danger and with an emperor far less secure in his position. In short, the Romans were acutely aware that any overall loss to Boudicca in Britannia would have been absolutely disastrous for them. You can see this in their response after Paulinus' final victory. This included drafting in 2,000 more legionaries from Germany together with 1,000 auxiliary cavalry and eight units of auxiliary foot to help stamp out the last flames of resistance to their occupation. This was then carried out with such vigour in the Iceni homelands of north Norfolk that the region remained for many years under-developed compared to the rest of the province.

BELOW
Rome's conquest of Britannia was nearly upended by Boudicca's rebellion

THE POSSIBILITY

61 CE – PRESENT

A VERY DIFFERENT POLITICAL LANDSCAPE

Without the stability of Roman rule across the country, and tribes all following their own way of life, disputing their territories and settling regional feuds, a Roman departure would have left the country far more fragmented. It's even possible that the countries we know as England, Scotland and Wales would have taken far longer to emerge, or even not exist at all. The gradual emergence from all the regional tribes of a dominant kingdom that could grow into a single unified nation would have been much more difficult, leading to centuries of instability and almost constant regional wars.

61 CE – PRESENT

MUD HUTS NOT METROPOLIS

Roman Britain created the foundations of modern life, with towns and cities of stone buildings, well-connected by efficient roads criss-crossing the country. With a Roman withdrawal the regional tribes may well have settled back into their own traditional ways, even purposefully rejecting any Roman influence. The emergence of towns and cities may have taken many more centuries, and perhaps in a less structured way. With the empire's stay cut short by centuries its legacy and influence would now be a very faint and almost insignificant influence on Britain's development.

61 CE – PRESENT

KING, WHAT KING?

With political instability following a Roman withdrawal the likelihood of a strong ruler to unify the feuding tribes, each with its own king, into a single country under one ruler would have been far more remote. The very concept of monarchy and kingship as we know it today may well have taken many more centuries to develop and take hold. Rome itself developed into an imperial empire with a single family lineage at its head and this became the model for all future generations of rulers to follow. Without the example of the Romans, there may never have been Alfred the Great, the long line of Saxon kings, or the subsequent monarchs that were to rule over an increasingly unified country.

What if...

ABLE ARCHER 83 HAD TURNED TO WAR?

With NATO mounting a training exercise for launching a nuclear strike, the Soviet Union thought it was the real thing and prepared to retaliate

INTERVIEW WITH

Taylor Downing

Taylor is a historian, writer, broadcaster and author of *1983 – The World at the Brink* and *1942 – Britain at the Brink*, on the military disasters and political crises of 1942.

As a regular NATO exercise, Able Archer was the supreme war game: to play out the processes of taking the US and NATO forces into a nuclear war with the Soviet Union. But 1983 was no ordinary year, with tension and mistrust between the two nuclear superpowers reaching dangerous levels. On the night of 9 November 1983, convinced Able Archer was cover to launch a real attack, Yuri Andropov, the ill and paranoid Soviet leader, placed his finger firmly on the nuclear button ready to push the whole planet into nuclear oblivion.

How different was the Cold War in 1983 to previous decades?
It's easy to see the Cold War as one continuous, unchanging period of ideological and political confrontation; in fact, there were many different phases to it. Coming out of WWII, the initial tensions and descent of the Iron Curtain came when the US still had a monopoly in nuclear weapons. But when the Soviet Union caught up and tested its own atomic bomb in 1949, the balance of power became more like a balance of terror. Throughout the 1950s both sides built up vast nuclear arsenals and exploded ever bigger thermonuclear bombs. This culminated in the Cuban Missile Crisis of October 1962, when the US and Soviet Union tried to stare each other down over the siting of Soviet nuclear missiles in Cuba. After this, Washington and Moscow realised they had to 'cool it' to avoid another direct confrontation. There followed, slowly at first but then with more momentum, a period of détente. This was symbolised by the docking in space of the Apollo and Soyuz space missions in 1975 and the collaboration of US and Soviet astronauts in joint exercises above the Earth. But by the end of the 1970s this détente was breaking down and both sides were growing suspicious of each other.

What role did the US and Soviet leaders take in raising tensions and what agendas did they have? Could this have influenced how military exercises were done?
Ronald Reagan became president in 1981 on a strongly anti-Soviet ticket. He believed the Soviets had used the years of détente as an opportunity to re-arm. Reagan called the Soviet Union "an evil empire" and talked about building a protective shield over North America to intercept incoming missiles, his 'Star Wars' initiative. This would have given the United States a huge advantage over the Soviets. The central belief of the Cold War was of Mutual Assured Destruction (MAD) – that neither side would attack the other with nuclear weapons because they knew there would be instant retaliation and it would be an act of suicide. But if you could protect your own country from missiles then there would be a greater temptation to launch a first strike.

RIGHT
Soviet SS-20 ICBMs were in place and ready for launch

What if...
ABLE ARCHER 83 HAD TURNED TO WAR?

71

What if... ABLE ARCHER 83 HAD TURNED TO WAR?

THE PAST

1981
STAR WARS AND THE 'EVIL EMPIRE'
Ronald Reagan won the White House with strong hardline rhetoric against the Soviet Union. They were the "Evil Empire" and the complete opposite of all America stood for. The Soviets had been falling behind the US in the technology stakes, and with the proposed Strategic Defence Initiative (a satellite-based anti-missile system nicknamed 'Star Wars'), the US would be able to shoot down Soviet warheads before they could reach their targets. Mutual Assured Destruction, which had kept the balance of nuclear power, no longer seemed mutual or assured. The Soviet Union started to see the US bogeyman around every corner.

1981-83
OPERATION RYAN
Yuri Andropov, head of the KGB (and soon to be the Soviet leader), and the rest of the Soviet hierarchy were convinced that Reagan's administration was planning a surprise pre-emptive nuclear strike. Under the codename RYAN, a huge information gathering exercise began, using agents and resources all around the globe. They tracked the movements and behaviour of those closest to the decision-making process for a nuclear first-strike, looking for clues to what they had already convinced themselves was the American plan. They were so convinced, it led to a tragic accident that raised the political temperature almost to boiling point.

SEPTEMBER 1983
TRIGGER-HAPPY TRAGEDY
US military bombers had played cat and mouse with Soviet airspace on many occasions, turning away at the last minute to test the radar tracking and defence responses. This only fuelled the Soviet belief of a surprise attack and, when a Korean Airlines Boeing 747 made navigation errors and crossed into Soviet airspace, jets were scrambled. Jumbled communication and obsession over a US first strike were to prove fatal, and KAL 007 was shot down by two air-to-air missiles. The hawks in the White House wanted an immediate military response, to no avail. It was to be two months later that the world was to stand on the edge of the abyss.

In the early 1980s the Kremlin leadership knew they were falling behind the West both economically and – more crucially – technologically. They came to believe that Reagan's aggressive language and US technological superiority betrayed a desire to launch a first strike against them. They grew paranoid, looking for signs of an imminent attack everywhere. By 1983 the Soviet leaders were feeling very edgy and tense.

Was Able Archer 83 more provocative than previous exercises to purposefully take things to the brink with the USSR?
Able Archer was a regular NATO exercise held every couple of years to rehearse the protocols for launching nuclear weapons. Every exercise was different but in essence it was a war game in which NATO faced defeat in a conventional war with the Warsaw Pact as Soviet and East European tanks came thrusting across into Western Europe. NATO responded by asking the political leadership for permission to launch nuclear weapons. Quite often the politicians in London and Washington DC took part in the exercise – they also had to know what to do should such a request ever be made to them. But in 1983 it was decided that the situation was too tense and so neither President Reagan nor Prime Minister Margaret Thatcher were involved. So no, Able Archer 1983 was not intended to be any more provocative than usual.

In 1983 was an 'accidental war' more or less likely? And were the fail-safe systems, especially the human element, enough to avoid it?
It was a supremely dangerous year in which a series of events seriously raised the temperature between East and West. Most obvious was the shooting down of a Korean civilian airliner, flight KAL 007, by a Soviet fighter plane on 1 September after it'd strayed off course by about 560km and ended up crossing Soviet airspace above a sensitive military area. Reagan couldn't believe this was a case of mistaken identity, a tragic accident that caused the deaths of 269 innocent people. He called the Soviet Union "a terrorist state" that showed no regard for human life.

I argue that at this point the Cold War nearly went 'hot' as some in Washington demanded a military retaliation against the Soviet Union. When situations are this tense it is always possible that one side will misinterpret what the other side is doing. In the end, the safety of all nuclear systems is reliant upon the human factor – it is a politician or military leader who finally has to respond to threats perceived or real and press the nuclear button. So no matter how sophisticated the fail-safe systems are, it is down to a person to make the final decision – and all humans are fallible.

Could the events leading up to Able Archer 83 be seen as an example of fake news and 'convenient' intelligence to suit a purpose? Or just a lack of competence?
There was genuine tension between the two superpowers in 1983. Both were deeply suspicious of the other and both believed that events confirmed their own understanding of the hostility or irresponsibility of the other side.

This was made worse by the lack of any effective communication between the superpower rivals. The Soviets had no real understanding of how Reagan and his administration thought and whether they were genuinely hostile to them or just acting up. Likewise, the Washington leaders and the

ABOVE
The annual Autumn Forge exercise (of which Able Archer was a part) had been run by NATO since the 1960s. Pictured here is the 1969 operation

intelligence community in the US had absolutely no idea of how paranoid and fearful the Soviet leaders had become and how vulnerable they felt. What every state needs from its intelligence establishment is an understanding of how the other side is likely to behave – especially if it is about to launch an attack upon you. But neither the CIA nor the KGB had the slightest understanding of the other. This is a real lesson for today. If we have no idea how, say, the leaders of North Korea or Iran are thinking then the possibility for misunderstanding is immense.

What if the Soviets had reacted to Able Archer 83 with conventional weapons either through choice or accident? Was a conventional conflict a possibility and would it have automatically escalated to nuclear?
Throughout the decades of Cold War, the United States and the Soviet Union were careful never to confront each other directly. Their hostility to each other was expressed through a series of 'proxy wars'. Each side would arm and equip an ally but avoid directly confronting the other side. These proxy wars took place in Africa (in Angola and Ethiopia), in Latin America (the Contras versus the Sandinistas in Nicaragua) and most obviously in the Middle East (Israel versus the Arab states). The Yom Kippur War of October 1973 produced a particularly tense moment when the US military was put on to a maximum state of alert and readiness. Even when the US was directly involved in a war (as in Korea or Vietnam) the Soviets were very careful not to give overt support to their enemies.

So, in my mind, any conventional war fought directly between the two superpowers would always have escalated into a nuclear confrontation. As soon as one side gained an advantage over the other, the side that felt it was losing would have had no alternative but to resort to the nuclear option. It is impossible to imagine that open conflict between Washington and Moscow could ever have remained a purely conventional war. It would almost certainly have led to a nuclear holocaust.

TOP
Pershing II missiles could reach Moscow within minutes

ABOVE
President Reagan's rhetoric fuelled Soviet suspicions of a surprise attack

THE POSSIBILITY

9 NOV 1983

FIRST BLOOD
Both sides had plans for limited nuclear strikes against missile sites or military bases, but it is inconceivable that it would have ended there. It is possible that Soviet first strikes might have been made against Western Europe and US strikes against Eastern European targets, leaving the principal protagonists untouched. But the pressure to avenge the total destruction of an ally meant war would've escalated. And likewise if, for instance, the Soviets had destroyed a single American city, like Atlanta, Georgia, and the US had only nuked Minsk in Belarus, it would never have ended there.

10 NOV 1983

MAD, MAD, MAD
There could be no winner of a nuclear war. Very few living things would have survived a nuclear exchange between the superpowers. These attacks would have triggered massive retaliation using the vast nuclear arsenals possessed by both superpowers, resulting in the Mutual Assured Destruction that had previously kept the peace for so long. Tens if not hundreds of millions of men, women and children would have died as a direct result of the huge destruction caused by nuclear explosions. Some American military leaders boasted they could blast the Soviet Union back into the Stone Age, but in truth neither side would have escaped such a fate.

DEC 1983

NOWHERE TO HIDE
It was well known at the time that a nuclear exchange would have thrown so much radiation into the atmosphere that this would have blown around the world, bringing what was called a 'nuclear winter' to the whole planet. Clouds of radioactive rain would have blown from continent to continent, crops would have failed, and people would have suffered from radiation sickness in parts of the world like southern Africa or Australasia that had not suffered direct nuclear hits.

What if...

SULEIMAN I HAD SEIZED VIENNA?

Local leaders look to make peace with new power in the region, but Charles V vows to reconquer the Austrian capital for Christendom

INTERVIEW WITH

Professor Nancy Bisaha

Professor Bisaha is the Professor of History and Director of Medieval and Renaissance Studies at Vassar College in New York, with a specialisation in the early Ottoman Empire.

What was the situation leading up to the Siege of Vienna in 1529?
You have this period of enormous build-up. [There was] a significant period of build-up under Mehmed II, who reigned from 1451 to 1481, and then after him his son Bayezid II, [and] then you have following him this important period of development with Selim I and his main area of interest [being] Egypt and the Holy Land, the Levant, Syria, that region. And that provided an enormous amount of new territory for the Ottomans and a new source of income and taxes and such. And then when you get to Suleiman, he inherits all of that and starts his reign in the 1520s. And he's looking again with greater interest at Eastern Europe. And one of the things that he does that is seen as important to the lead up is his attempt to conquer Hungary. So the Battle of Mohács takes place in 1526 and he's able to conquer roughly half of Hungary. But of course the other half of the country continues to resist and they're working with the Habsburgs and others to try to throw them out, trying to push them out. So that's seen as one of the reason why Suleiman decides to attack Vienna.

Why was the Siege of Vienna ultimately unsuccessful?
There are a few factors that played into it. One is that they were very far from their centre of supply. They had marched out much farther west than they had before. They were in constant threat of being cut off from their supply lines. It was also an incredibly rainy period, so moving the troops under these conditions was very difficult. Keeping them together and keeping up morale was very hard. They faced issues like the gunpowder getting wet. It didn't have as many factors in its favour as some of the other sieges that ultimately were more successful.

What was the outcome of losing the siege?
One big theory is that this caused the Ottomans to shift their focus away a

RIGHT
After losing the battle, the Ottomans focused on the Mediterranean

What if...
SULEIMAN I HAD SEIZED VIENNA?

What if... SULEIMAN I HAD SEIZED VIENNA?

little bit from Eastern Europe. That they were going to try to expand their empire very much in that region after that. It made them look a little more toward the Mediterranean. They're much more active in that area, as far as North Africa and other places like that, so that's one aspect. But the other aspect is you could say that arguably, if Suleiman's goal was to protect Hungary, it achieved that goal. There weren't any serious threats to it, certainly coming by way of Central Europe or the Habsburgs after that. That did help stabilise the region for him for quite some time.

What if the Ottomans had successfully conquered Vienna?

It would have been seen as an incredible victory, but also it would have added to some of their challenges, because of the distance from the centre of the empire. I think they would have always been worried about being surrounded, being cut off from their supplies, from regular access to replenishment of troops and other resources from the centre of the administration. So I think they would have had to work very hard to secure the area around Vienna, and all the routes leading back toward the East. That would have cost them a lot, in addition to the outlay of the conquest itself. The maintenance would have been very high. That, plus all of the pressures they were facing from the Safavids [in Persia] and others, that could have led to a lot of fragmentation. They might have found that they had overstretched if they'd won.

What would Ottoman victory have meant for Europe?

One thing the Ottomans were doing, that Christian cities weren't, is the Ottoman cities were more integrated. You had not just Muslims, but Christians and Jews, and they were all an active part of these towns in Europe. That might have been very eye-opening for Europeans to experience that, for central Europeans in particular. You could make the argument, had they held on to Vienna and other areas around it, it might have created a greater acceptance of who the Ottomans were, and allowed more people to see them as fellow rulers in the area, to understand their strategies a little bit better. The anti-Ottoman rhetoric just [kept] getting stronger and stronger. It's easy to do that once someone is located a distance away from you, right? It's easier to vilify them and to indulge in a lot of stereotypes and such, but when they're living much closer by and you're dealing with them, as fellow rulers, as neighbours in your own town, as trade associates, it often times is much more eye-opening.

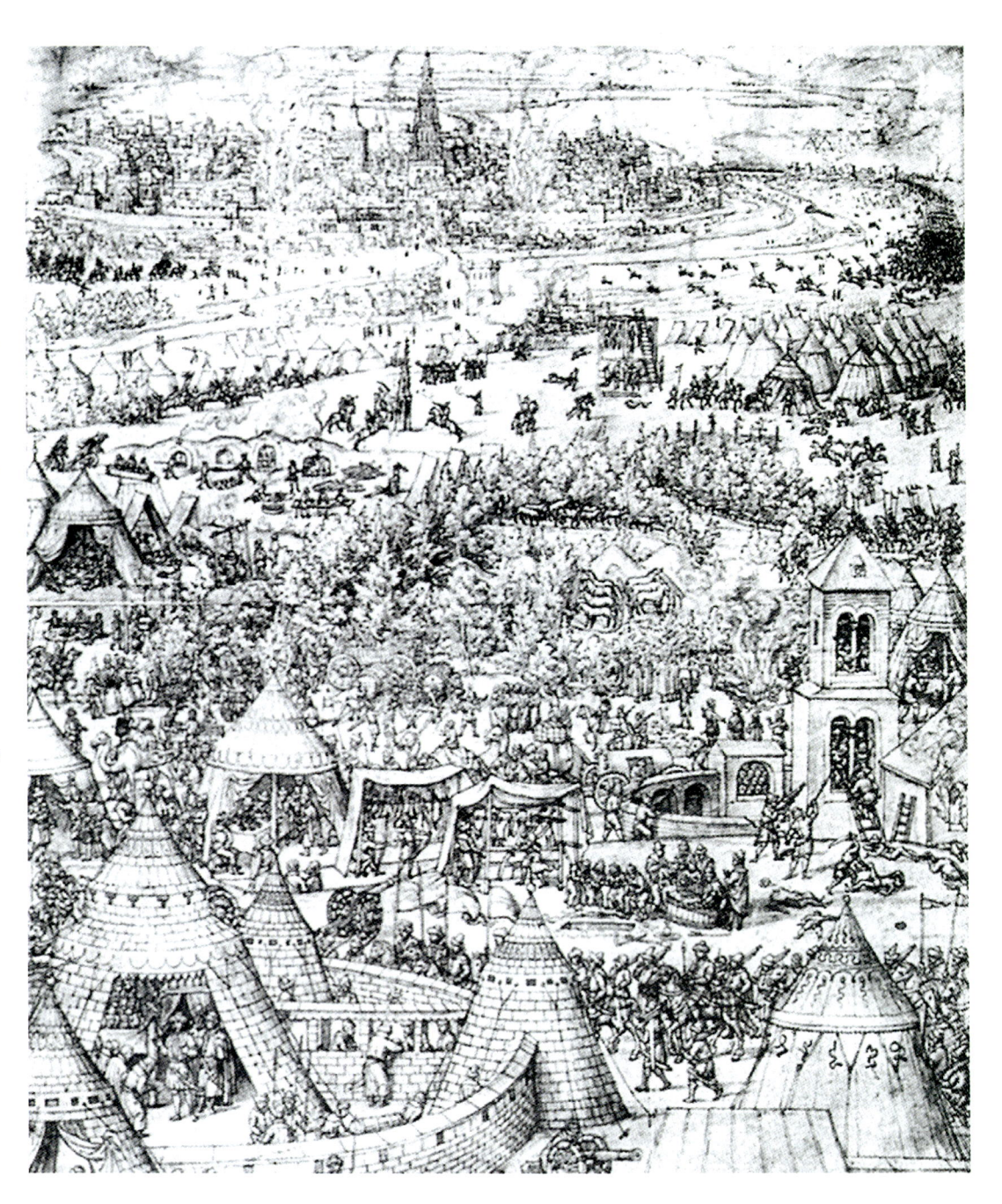

What implications does that have in the longer term?

It would have made the Ottoman Empire more of a familiar partner in European politics. There are two kinds of tracks that you see in the way that people were dealing with the Ottomans in Eastern Europe. One was to be outraged that this foreign power, this Muslim power, was ruling over formerly Christian areas and to say this was unacceptable and they had to be expelled and they didn't belong there. The other was to deal with them, and accept them to open up diplomatic lines, which most governments did immediately. Once you get behind some of the rhetoric about the Ottomans as being 'the infidel', or 'the barbarian', as they were also called at this time, they're treated like other local princes. So it might have lessened a lot of the fear, that sense of distance that developed about Islam and Muslims. It might have reduced that sense of othering that you see toward Islam, and of there being a divide between East and West. I think it could have really softened that, if they had a much stronger presence in central Europe. That I think is very possible.

Would the Ottomans have tried to conquer the whole of Europe?

I'm sceptical about that. I think they would have run out of steam. I think they would have been hard-pressed to really keep

ABOVE
The Ottomans were ultimately forced to withdraw and admit defeat

RIGHT
The Ottomans tried and failed to take Vienna again in 1683

> "It might have reduced that sense of othering that you see toward Islam"

going on, given how greatly the Ottoman Empire had expanded all over the place. I don't know if they would have had the wherewithal to keep going, because I think the resistance would have been enormous. Even if some people did cooperate with the Ottomans, there would have been just tremendous push-back. I mean, Charles V [the King of Spain] would not have settled for letting Vienna go. He'd have worked very hard to get it back, so I think that that would have been one immediate response.

Would there have been a lot of additional conflict?
I think the Ottomans were an aggressive state. They were expansive. They wanted to continue to expand their empire. I don't think it makes a lot of sense to say they were completely peaceful rulers. So I think they had very clear goals in mind. It's a different question as to whether they could have kept going, but if they had all the resources, given their past history, I think there's a lot of reason to expect they would have. That was kind of part of what they did.

Would Europe have been better or worse off if they had won?
I think it certainly would have been bad for a lot of the rulers in Europe. They would have lost a lot of power, they would have lost direct control. The Ottomans ruled over multicultural, multi-religious empires, so many people continued to practise their faith. They kept their own sense of local culture and practices. They had a lot of autonomy under the Ottomans in many areas. They could run a lot of their own businesses and [set] agendas on their own. I don't know if you were to ask somebody, a Christian living in the Ottoman Empire in Eastern Europe, if they felt like it was a great hardship, if you would have gotten the answer of yes. They probably looked at it more in terms of this was an empire that, once they established their goals, was pretty well-run, was well-maintained. The roads were protected. They brought a lot of peace after war, so the argument's been made by a lot of historians that in some cases people thought they lived as well, if not better, under the Ottomans.

Suleiman's man in Hungary

Ottoman interest in Europe began long before its attempts to seize Vienna from the Holy Roman Empire. Prior to this they had fought over Hungary and even successfully installed their own king to the region, John Zápolya. Descended from a noble Slavonian family, Zápolya was already rich and powerful having inherited land in what is now Slovakia from his father, yet he still had his eye firmly on the throne. When King Louis II was killed at the Battle of Mohács, Zápolya attempted to step into the void left by the heirless king, but faced competition from Archduke Ferdinand of Austria for the position.

When Ferdinand's brother the Holy Roman Emperor Charles V invaded Hungary, Zápolya was forced into exile. He turned to Suleiman I for support, promising Hungary as a vassal state to the Ottoman Empire in return, which lead directly to Suleiman laying siege to Vienna.

King John originally named Ferdinand his heir to make peace, but then had a son and left the Kingdom of Hungary to him

77

What if...

JAPAN HAD REFUSED TO SURRENDER?

Massive invasions by the Americans and the Soviets planned after first-ever atomic bomb attacks fail to dent Japan's resolve

INTERVIEW WITH

Professor Robert Pape

Robert Pape is Professor of Political Science at the University of Chicago. He is an expert in international security affairs, and in 1993 published a detailed journal article on Japan's surrender in WWII.

What was the background to the US dropping two atomic bombs on Japan in August 1945?
[The US] defeated Germany in the spring of 1945 and then started to really focus on Japan. That became the main theatre of war. And as the summer continued, it became clear that the city bombings of Japan and the military pressures that we were putting Japan under were not going to be enough. It wasn't clear exactly what the future was going to be. And we had meetings with the Soviets at Potsdam in July, and it became very clear that the Soviets were going to launch a ground defence within Manchuria against the Japanese army. And that set of meetings then essentially made it clear that if the United States was going to play a role, that it was the atomic bomb that was really going to be the option here.

Why did Japan announce its decision to surrender on 15 August 1945?
The first atomic bomb actually is not generating much pressure on the Japanese political leaders to surrender. The key obstacle it turns out, which we did not know at the time, was the Japanese army. [Korechika] Anami, the top general of the Japanese army, was the most resistant to any surrender. And, after we dropped the first bomb on Hiroshima, there's actually a continued logjam. And then on the night of 8 August, that's when the Soviet Union launches this massive invasion into Manchuria. And it is just a crushing blow. They just are piercing right through the Japanese army like a hot knife through butter, and within hours [the Japanese army is] just cut to pieces. They're not able to put up any organised resistance. About 12 hours after the Soviet invasion happened, that's when we dropped the second bomb and that's when Anami stops putting up resistance. He essentially stopped vetoing the surrender. It's Anami's decision that really leads to the surrender, and that veto is tightly linked to the Soviet invasion.

How did Japan's surrender play out?
[After the Soviet invasion] the whole plan for the home island defence now was completely worthless. And that's when Anami just stops resisting. And then he goes even further about a day later, because the Japanese army had a plan that if the emperor were to surrender without their agreement, that they were going to kill the emperor and replace them with Anami. Well, Anami commits hara-kiri [a form of suicide], and that prevents the military plan from being executed. He decapitates that plan so that the surrender actually happens. And then on 15 August, that's when the emperor announces the surrender. And it's a really important event that speech for the surrender, because all the resistance essentially ends. That's really the turning point where there's just no resistance.

What would the Americans have done if Japan hadn't surrendered?
We know what would have happened in the very next month or so. There are four home islands of Japan. Kyushu is the southernmost island. That was going to be the target of the first invasion. And that was going to happen sometime in that early fall, 1945, had Japan not surrendered. When the Soviets invaded Manchuria and

RIGHT
Japan formally signed its surrender on 2 September 1945

What if...
JAPAN HAD REFUSED TO SURRENDER?

What if... JAPAN HAD REFUSED TO SURRENDER?

THE PAST

7 DECEMBER 1941

OUT OF THE BLUE
The US naval base at Pearl Harbor in Hawaii is attacked by Japanese forces. The Japanese had already occupied all of Indochina and had entered into an alliance with Germany and Italy. Commerce agreements had been cancelled and Japanese goods under embargo. Negotiations were taking place but getting nowhere. With the first Japanese wave, US planes were attacked on the ground. More than 150 were destroyed. In the harbour, with the fleet moored for the weekend, almost 20 ships were sunk or damaged. Around 2,400 military personnel were killed and over 1,145 injured. Although humiliated by the attack, it galvanised the American people behind going to war.

1942-43

ACROSS THE PACIFIC
Following Pearl Harbor, the Japanese forces pressed ahead with the occupation of a huge area of the Pacific. The Allied forces aimed to contain the Japanese, keep supply lines open and counterattack with amphibious forces. Following the Battle of the Coral Sea, the Battle of Midway became a pivotal moment and caused serious damage to Japanese forces and morale. The Battle of Guadalcanal was six months of attack and counterattack with losses on both sides. Eventually the US Army and Marines won through, and the American and Australian forces began to retake territory.

1943-45

THE END IS NIGH
After Guadalcanal Japan realised it was on the defensive, its forces stretched. Rabaul was encircled and neutralised. Japan's Eastern flank was vulnerable. With the fall of Saipan in the Marianas, bombers could reach Japan itself. Guam was to follow, and then Tinian, the base of the Enola Gay. Iwo Jima was small but significant, and one of the hardest fought battles of the campaign, but it was secured. The invasion of Okinawa was the largest amphibious landing of the entire Pacific war. Japanese cities were now being firebombed on a regular basis. The defeat of Japan from the air seemed possible. It was to take the destruction of Hiroshima and Nagasaki by a terrifying new weapon for Japan to accept it was beaten.

> "There weren't the atomic bombs to drop. The US only had two more"

just wiped [the Japanese army] to pieces, this showed that the Japanese army's plan for homeland defence was a non-starter. Japan fully realised that [the US] were building an invasion force. We were doing an island-hopping campaign, and we were bringing to bear hundreds of thousands of troops that were going to be invading the home islands in just a short period of time, and Kyushu was the next target.

What would have happened next?
Had we invaded Kyushu, the US military did estimates of how long it would take, what the resistance would be and also the American casualties that would result from the invasion and occupation of Kyushu. And essentially 50,000 Americans would likely have died just to take Kyushu. Hundreds of thousands of Japanese would have died in that. Then what would have likely happened after that is the brute force conquest island by island of the four islands, where Honshu would probably have been next, where Tokyo is and so forth. There has been speculation ever since we dropped the bomb of what the American casualties would have been to take Honshu, and the numbers that are bandied about are like a half million Americans dead. But that's more of a guesstimate than an actual estimate, because the detailed planning for taking Honshu had not happened yet.

Would the US have dropped more atomic bombs?
Well, we only had two more, so we had a limited stockpile. We only were going to have two more bombs by December 1945. People who don't know the historical details of the case would just naturally assume, oh America could drop dozens or hundreds of atomic bombs on Japan. In fact, American opinion polls at the time when Japan surrendered [showed] that 22 or 25 per cent of Americans wanted us to keep bombing using the atomic bombs even after Japan surrendered, because we were pretty angry about Pearl Harbor. But there weren't the bombs to drop. There were two more, but it would have taken many months here to produce a large number of atomic bombs. And we had already destroyed most of the cities anyway. So, by the time we dropped the atomic bombs, half of the cities' urban areas had already been completely erased and obliterated by firebombings.

Would there have been a race to conquer Japan between the Soviet Union and the US, similar to the race to Berlin in Germany?

TOP LEFT
The US planned to conquer Japan island by island

LEFT
General Anami was part of a coup to overthrow the Emperor

ABOVE
News of Japan's surrender was celebrated across Europe

A slower race, yeah. Just as we are doing amphibious landings on the home islands, the Soviets would be in a position of taking control of large parts of the Japanese-controlled mainland, and then do their own amphibious landings as well. It would've been a months-long slogging campaign, six to eight months at a minimum, to move through those four home islands. And that would've been true for either the American side or the Soviet side. And it's something that would have been a massive undertaking, because amphibious operations are just fantastically difficult to do. We had to do one giant amphibious operation in Europe, that was in Normandy at Omaha Beach. The Japanese theatre is a whole series of amphibious operation after amphibious operation.

Would we have seen a divided Japan like we saw a divided Germany?
It's possible. The risk of direct conflict between the United States and the Soviet Union would have been much more direct, because given that the Soviets would have to do amphibious operations and we have a very significant navy and naval blockade of Japan. What we would be doing as we're taking Kyushu is we would be tightening the blockade around the four home islands even tighter. And that would not only prevent any access of shipping into Japan, but it would also directly impede any possible amphibious operation by the Soviets. So I think that what you would have seen is, unlike what's happening in the race to Berlin [at] the middle of Germany, where there's no possibility of Americans shooting Soviets, I think the risk here of a confrontation with the Soviets is much more real. So rather than a divided Japan like you saw a divided West Germany and East Germany, I think it's more that there could have been more direct confrontation with the Soviets.

What impact would this have had on Europe?
The United States after the surrender of Japan could refocus a lot of its efforts on Europe, which is what we did. However, had we not, had we had to have that brute force island-by-island conquest of Japan, that would have created a real tension between dealing with Japan and then shifting over to Europe. It would have kept our focus on the Far East and it would've done that for many months, if not several years. I think that you would have had much less economic focus on Western Europe. I think this would've put at risk the Marshall Plan. It would have opened the door to much more Soviet influence in Western Europe than actually occurred. And even the whole idea that NATO would have come together in 1949, it just raises lots of questions about whether that would have actually happened. That whole giant effort to forcibly conquer the Japanese home islands would have had some pretty big reverberations in terms of the history of Europe.

THE POSSIBILITY

1945-46

ISLAND HOPPING
The dropping of the atomic bombs on Hiroshima and Nagasaki was the ultimate in sending a message of superior power to the enemy. In that sense it did its job, and the resulting Japanese surrender saved a prolonged war and many more lives. But it was not a campaign. There were not stockpiles of atomic bombs waiting to be used. Two, at least for the time being, was it. Had Japan not surrendered then the planned ground invasion would have been put into operation. Except that it was not just one piece of ground to invade and capture, it was four main islands making up the core of Japan.

1945

FIGHTING OVER THE SCRAPS
Having revoked its neutrality pact with Japan, Russia could now regard itself as an open player in the Far East. Although allies of the US in Europe against Hitler, Stalin may now feel it possible to make some gains on his Eastern flank. With the US conducting amphibious landings from the East, and the Russians invading from the North and West, the potential for a misunderstanding, or even intentional engagement between the two forces would increase. In defeat, Japan could become a battleground – military or political – between two powers eager to secure their influence in the region and gain essential global kudos over their rival.

1945 ONWARDS

EUROPE COMES SECOND
A prolonged war against Japan would have had a significant impact on the resources and manpower of the Allies. By keeping troops in the field for longer the drains on domestic finances would have become substantial. Also, with a financially costly land assault on the Japanese mainland inevitable, any support given by the US to the aftermath of the war in Europe would have been minimal, as would a continued US presence there. The Soviet Union, however, may decide not to become too embroiled in the execution of Japan's defeat, choosing instead to focus on Europe and what it could gain, materially and influentially, without the overarching impact of the US in its way.

What if...

THE CHINESE COMMUNISTS HAD LOST?

The communist takeover of China in 1949 helped shape the Cold War and the modern world, but what if they'd lost?

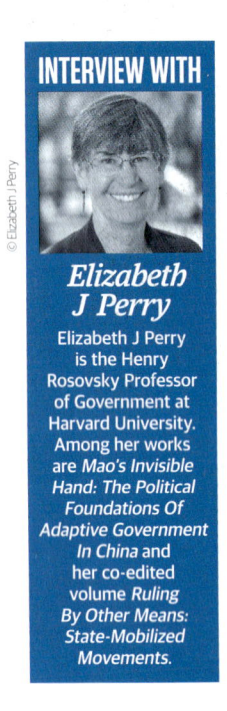

INTERVIEW WITH

Elizabeth J Perry

Elizabeth J Perry is the Henry Rosovsky Professor of Government at Harvard University. Among her works are *Mao's Invisible Hand: The Political Foundations Of Adaptive Government In China* and her co-edited volume *Ruling By Other Means: State-Mobilized Movements*.

What was the situation in China leading up to the communist takeover in 1949?

China, on the eve of the communist takeover, was in terrible shape. The ruling KMT [Nationalist Party] government had descended into corruption on many levels and there was galloping inflation. China, of course, had been very hard hit by the Japanese invasion that began in the late-1930s. That had ended only in 1945 and so it was still a war-torn country, impoverished, with tremendous inequality, political disorder and poor public health. There was a great deal of unhappiness on the part of many different sectors of the population with respect to the KMT regime. Initially, when the nationalists unified China in 1927-1928, there was considerable hope that they would really usher in a kind of new age for China. However, after the Japanese invasion more and more people, including the intelligentsia, as well as the peasantry, went over to the communist side, for patriotic as well as pragmatic reasons. There was a realization that the Nationalists were not fighting the Japanese or managing the economy effectively, and that the country was in danger of permanently losing its sovereignty.

Who was Mao Zedong and the CCP?

Mao came from Hunan Province in the heartland of China and was born in what he later characterised as a rich peasant family. He was educated primarily in a traditional Chinese way with Chinese classics, which helps explain why he later became a very successful poet as well as an essayist. While working as a librarian at Peking University, he felt that he was looked down upon by the more elite Chinese intellectuals because he retained certain peasant-like traits. The primary co-founders of the Chinese Communist Party [CCP] were two other intellectuals active at Peking University at the same time. One was the director of the library, Li Dazhao, and the other was the dean, Chen Duxiu. Due in part to their invitation, Mao attended the founding of the party in 1921. His first assignment was to organise workers in his native Hunan Province, but he quickly realised that the peasantry more than the workers were going to have to be the main social force of revolution and he became the head of the peasant bureau. Mao was not recognised as the paramount leader of the Chinese Communist Party until the Long March that took the communists out of their Jiangxi Soviet base all the way up to the northwest to Yan'an in Shaanxi Province. It was during this period (1930s-1940s) that Mao began to articulate what we think of as Maoism – a distinctive recipe for revolution focused on peasant mobilisation and guerrilla warfare against an overwhelming enemy.

Who exactly were their main opponents, the KMT?

The KMT, also known as the Nationalists, trace their roots back to activists in the 1911 revolution that brought down China's last imperial dynasty. The KMT established its capital in Nanjing in 1927 after defeating warlords who ruled China at the time. By this point, the head of the KMT was Chiang Kai-shek. In cooperation with members of secret societies in the industrial city of Shanghai, he brutally attacked the communist labour movement there in the spring of 1927. This was an

RIGHT A Chinese communist rally in 1932

What if...
THE CHINESE COMMUNISTS HAD LOST?

What if... THE CHINESE COMMUNISTS HAD LOST?

THE PAST

1949
COMMUNIST REVOLUTION
Following four years of civil war in China, the CCP took control. After the CCP's formation in 1921, the massacre of many of its members by the nationalists in 1927 and years of tenuous partnerships with those same groups, the nationalists were forced to flee. Following this there were numerous executions as Mao asserted his authority.

1958-1960
THE GREAT LEAP FORWARD
A campaign launched in 1958 by Mao to bring industry to the countryside, which included, among other things, 'backyard furnaces' to help steel output. Misguided policies such as 'sparrowcide' (massacring all sparrows to protect crops, not taking into account the insects they eat) and a desire by local officials to complete quotas (collecting 'surpluses' that did not exist) led to widespread famine.

1960
SINO-SOVIET SPLIT
Following the death of Stalin, Nikita Krushchev lead the Soviet Union. Due to tensions between himself and Chairman Mao, he withdrew all technical aid and support from China.

1966-1976
CULTURAL REVOLUTION
Following the Great Leap Forward, Mao stepped down from his position of power. However in 1966 he called on the youth to rebel against capitalist and traditionalist movements in society – while simultaneously removing his enemies from within the CCP. Numerous intellectuals were tortured and killed, with the figures ranging anywhere from hundreds of thousands to 20 million.

---

important turning point in the history of Chinese communism, causing the communists to move out of the cities into the countryside. So the KMT were opponents, but also periodic allies of the Chinese communists, having jointly fought warlords in the 1920s and allying again during World War II to fight the Japanese. This second united front broke down toward the end of WWII, and after the Japanese withdrawal the communists engaged in civil war against the nationalists from 1945 to 1949.

How did the CCP finally gain control?
It was a two-fold process. On the one hand, the Communist Party was gaining more and more territory in the countryside. The Long March had begun as a defeat. However, after the Japanese invaded, the communists began to develop a successful guerrilla warfare strategy and gained increasingly more territory. At the same time the Japanese invasion helped to unravel the KMT. Corruption was rife in the KMT during World War II. Funds that were supposed to go toward fighting actually went into the pockets of various KMT leaders. By the end of World War II, the tables had turned and the communists gained the upper hand. The communists were able to gain control because of the implosion of the KMT, which proved unable to control the economy and unite the different warring factions within the Nationalist Party. The Battle of Huai-hai in 1948 was a critical juncture, after which a number of soldiers defected from the KMT side and went over to the communist side.

ABOVE KMT troops leaving Canton following defeat

What were some of the immediate effects of the communist takeover?
The communists carried out dramatic changes in the cities and countryside: land reform in the villages, socialisation of industry in the factories, thought reform in the universities. These were conducted as mass campaigns in which ordinary citizens were mobilized by the state to help implement its radical agenda. The campaigns were violent, with millions of landlords, rich peasants, KMT sympathisers, Japanese 'puppets', bandits, secret society members, sectarians, and other 'enemies of the people' killed. But inflation was brought under control and public order was largely restored through a series of draconian disciplinary measures. By the late 1950s, people were subject to a household registration system that severely limited mobility. Class labels were imposed to divide the population into 'good' classes like peasants and workers and 'bad' classes like landlords

> "Millions of landlords, rich peasants and other 'enemies of the people' were killed"

and rich peasants. It was a very, very different society from what China had looked like before the revolution.

Were there any points when the communists could have failed?

Before the outbreak of World War II, very few people would have expected a communist takeover in China. Had Chiang Kai-shek managed to tame the factional struggles within the KMT or to curb the rampant inflation and corruption, things could have gone very differently. Had the Japanese not invaded, it would surely have been a very different timetable if not an entirely different outcome. There was nothing preordained about the victory of the communist revolution, from 1921 when the CCP was founded until 1949 when it took over the mainland.

What could some of the effects for China have been had the communists been defeated?

Had the KMT managed to eliminate the communist threat during the civil war you might have seen a somewhat less coercive government, simply by virtue of the fact it was less powerful than the communists. But my guess is what would have happened is China would have limped along for a very

ABOVE Mao Zedong declaring the birth of communist China

BELOW Leader of the KMT, Chiang Kai-shek

substantial period of time. We can look at Taiwan and say, "Oh well, because Chiang Kai-shek set up a very successful regime he would have done the same on the mainland," but I think that's a very implausible comparison. Much of the reason the KMT was able to reform itself on Taiwan was precisely because it had just suffered such a disastrous defeat and had to reconsider everything. Had the KMT remained in power on the mainland, there would surely have been a lot of loss of life through neglect, disease, poverty, political disorder and so forth. However, you would likely not have seen the executions nor a famine of the sort that occurred under Mao during the Great Leap Forward. When Mao broke with the Soviet Union and tried to apply his own guerrilla tactics to develop the countryside, China experienced the worst famine in all of history, with tens of millions dying of starvation. But you would probably have seen the continuation for many years of all of those problems that had existed before the communist revolution.

What could some of the effects have been globally had the communists not succeeded?

Had the communists not won, the Soviet Union would not have been China's closest ally in the 1950s. The Cold War would obviously have been very different had the US and China remained allies. But surely the Soviets would have aided remnant communists and other would-be revolutionaries seeking to take advantage of KMT weakness. So it's hard to imagine that a communist loss in the civil war with the KMT would have ushered in a peaceful or stable situation.

THE POSSIBILITY

1949-1975

CHIANG KAI-SHEK AND TAIWAN

The leader of the KMT, Chiang Kai-shek immediately moved the government to Taiwan where he resumed his duties as President of the Republic of China. He consistently claimed sovereignty over all of China, as well as making preparations to retake the mainland. Kai-shek would finance insurgent groups and plan a full-scale invasion in 1962. While ruling Taiwan, he purged the party of what he saw as corrupt elements. In the 1950s American aid and a land-reform act led to the island becoming economically prosperous. This has led historians to wonder what the possible changes Kai-shek would have instigated had he been able to once again seize control of the mainland.

1949-1997

HONG KONG

Until 1997, Hong Kong remained under the rule of the British. Large numbers of refugees from China fled from the mainland during the initial communist takeover in 1949 and further numbers fled following the Great Leap Forward and Cultural Revolution. Hong Kong's history is intertwined with its British rule – had the KMT been able to win the civil war, it is possible it would have been returned to Chinese rule earlier.

1950s & 1960s

RELATIONSHIP WITH THE USA DURING THE COLD WAR

Chinese relations with the USA throughout the period of the Cold War were initially tense, having a much closer bond with the Soviet Union. The Korean War, Taiwan Strait Crisis, Vietnam War and Chinese atomic tests were just some of the events which led to a steady escalating of tensions throughout the 1950s and 1960s. Although relations improved in the 1970s, due in part to the Sino-Soviet Split, these earlier aggressions greatly affected the nature of the Cold War, particularly when China too became a nuclear power. Had the US allied more closely with a capitalist China, it is likely that the Cold War could have taken a vastly different path.

What if...

MEXICO HAD DEFEATED THE UNITED STATES?

What would have happened had Mexico maintained its claim on vast swathes of territory, including the potentially gold-rich California?

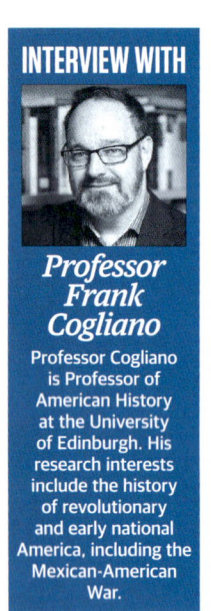

INTERVIEW WITH

Professor Frank Cogliano

Professor Cogliano is Professor of American History at the University of Edinburgh. His research interests include the history of revolutionary and early national America, including the Mexican-American War.

What was the background to the Mexican-American War of 1846-48?
The US in the early 19th century had a rapidly growing population, particularly in the west. [This] put it on a collision course with the Republic of Mexico, which had acquired its independence in the 1820s and claimed much of the territory in what is now the southwest of the United States, and indeed the Pacific Coast of the United States. So in the 1840s the US found itself on a potential road to conflict with both Mexico and Britain in what's today the Pacific Northwest. That's the big picture. The more proximate cause is that the American settlers in the Mexican province of Texas in 1836 rebelled, declared independence, fought a short but relatively bloody war of independence and achieved their independence. And then the United States, in 1846, annexed Texas, and that set the war in motion between 1846 and 1848.

What happened from 1846 to 1848?
The US and Mexico fought on a number of fronts. American troops invaded what we now think of as modern Mexico [through Texas]. Other American troops went west to California. And then, in probably the big campaign of the war, General Winfield Scott landed at Veracruz and actually went inland through the heart of Mexico, capturing Mexico City, which the Duke of Wellington called the greatest campaign in history. So the Americans invaded Mexico, or seized Mexican territory, on three fronts.

Was this a one-sided fight in favour of the Americans?
That's how it's often portrayed, in part because of the subsequent history about the wealth and strength of the two countries. But actually, it was much more equal than people often say, in the sense that Mexico had had its own revolution in the 1820s and actually had pretty sophisticated military forces, while the American army wasn't that good. It became better in the course of the war, but it was largely a volunteer force and there were a lot of state militias involved. So there was a lot of pretty bloody fighting. It was a relatively brief conflict, and the outcome appeared to be so one-sided because we see the power disparity historically between the United States and Mexico since. There's a tendency to kind of read that back, but it was a slightly closer thing than people often realise.

What were the outcomes of the war?
For the United States, the main outcome was that they acquired what's called the Mexican Cession, which was this massive amount of territory in the western part of North America. In 1848, with the Treaty of Guadalupe Hidalgo, the United States acquired most of the territory that's now in the western United States. I'm talking about Texas, of course, but [also] the states of New Mexico, Arizona, California, Nevada, Utah and so forth. This [set in motion] the chain of events that led to the American Civil War, because of the dispute between the North and South about whether the newly acquired territory should be slave territory or not.

Was there a turning point where the war could have swung the other way?
In some of the early battles that were fairly close, if Mexico had won those, maybe the United States wouldn't have pursued the campaign. It would have been very interesting if the Mexicans had held on to California, because of course we know that gold was discovered there. The United

RIGHT
General Winfield Scott leads his troops triumphantly into Mexico City

What if...
MEXICO HAD DEFEATED THE UNITED STATES?

What if... MEXICO HAD DEFEATED THE UNITED STATES?

RIGHT
Antonio López de Santa Anna originally opposed Mexican independence from Spain, but then supported it

BELLOW
President James Polk sought to expand US territory

States acquired California in 1848 in the Treaty of Guadalupe Hidalgo and then almost immediately gold was discovered. The Gold Rush of 1849 was set off. So if that territory had remained Mexican, and the gold had been in Mexico instead of a newly acquired territory of the United States, that might have been an important turning point.

What would a Mexican victory have meant for the expansion of the US?
If Mexico had been victorious and blocked the expansion of United States to the south and west, there were two possible outcomes. One is that American settlers would've continued going into Mexican territory to settle, because the population was doubling every generation. The United States had an incredibly rapidly growing population, both through an actual increase and through immigration. [Or] maybe United States and American settlers would not have gone to the west but into the northwest and Canada instead.

What would victory have meant for Mexico?
They were fighting to maintain their territorial integrity, [and] they were also concerned about the fate of their citizens. Mexico was a republic, too, and sought to protect the rights of its citizens in the territory that the United States coveted, especially in Texas, but then latterly in California and New Mexico. Mexico's claims to that territory were pretty good.

Would Mexico have abolished slavery in the American south?
It wouldn't have been able to abolish it across the American south. [But] it prohibited slavery in the province of Texas. There had been slavery in Mexico before independence, but one of the legacies of the Mexican Revolution in the 1820s was the abolition of slavery throughout Mexico. That was confirmed in Texas in the 1830s. The American settlers in Texas were bringing their slaves into their province, and that was one of the things that prompted the Texas Revolution, which eventually prompted the Mexican War. Ironically this westward expansion was going to end the debate over western expansionism. It was going to be a catalyst of the American Civil War, which of course, is about slavery.

Would the American Civil War have been less likely to happen?
Yes, in the short term. The acquisition of all that territory and the political controversy over whether that territory would be slave or free was a direct cause of the Civil War. The other thing was, militarily, a lot of the men who served as officers in the Mexican War went on to be officers and generals in the American Civil War on both sides. And if their experience was different, maybe the country would have been less willing to go to war. If they'd suffered a humiliating defeat, maybe in 1861 both sides would have been less willing to go to war. The lesson that many Americans drew from the Mexican War, which is incorrect in my view, is that war is pretty quick and easy and you can win decisively, and then the rewards follow.

What would it have meant for the Native American population in the western US?
Between 1865 and 1895, there was a series of Indian wars in the far west that

"Mexico had a sophisticated military, while the American army wasn't that good"

were pretty brutal and pretty one-sided in their outcome. That probably wouldn't have happened if Mexico had controlled that territory, at least probably not in the same way. There's a slight tendency where [people] assume Mexico is somehow benign when it comes to Native American relations. That's not true, but they were slightly less efficient at displacing native people from the United States. It's a sad tale of displacement and resistance, and it's certainly hard to imagine it being worse if Mexico won the Mexican War, that's for sure.

Would Mexico have had a Gold Rush?
The addition of capital as a result of the Gold Rush was kind of a steroid shot to the American economy. So if that had gone to Mexico, then Mexican development might have been different. One thing I would say is, one can imagine that if the United States had lost the Mexican War and then gold was discovered in California, maybe it would've gone to war with Mexico again in California.

What impact would there have been on US-Mexico relations?
A Mexican victory in this war might've changed the tone of US-Mexican relations which are, as we know, complicated to this very day, to some extent because of the legacy of this war. A huge proportion of the population of the western United States today are of Mexican descent and many of them feel a cultural affinity with Mexico. Many of them of course feel an affinity to the United States. Millions of them are citizens of the United States. But the war and the legacy of this war is a complicated one for both Mexico as a nation and for Mexican-Americans. If Mexico had won the war, then it's hard not to think that maybe at least some Americans would not have quite such a kind of paternalistic and patronizing view of Mexico.

Manifest Destiny

Prior to the annexation of Texas and the outbreak of the Mexican-American War, the concept of Manifest Destiny had begun to take hold across the United States, particularly within the Democratic Party of that time. The idea, originally proposed in the 1830s, was that the US had a duty to spread its way of life across the North American continent, establishing the supremacy of its ideals over those of the Old World its founders had previously defeated. Manifest Destiny was not without opponents, however, with many believing that it was merely a self-aggrandising cover for imperialism, which they rejected as an Old-World concept. Prominent figures in later years, such as Abraham Lincoln and Ulysses S Grant, were among those who rejected Manifest Destiny, with Grant (who fought in the Mexican-American War) calling the Mexican War "one of the most unjust ever waged by a stronger against a weaker nation."

John Gast's 1872 painting entitled 'Spirit of the Frontier' shows Columbia watching over settlers heading west

What if...

THE FIRST CRUSADE HAD BEEN DEFEATED?

How might the history of the Middle Ages have been altered had this massive event gone in a different direction?

INTERVIEW WITH

Peter Frankopan
Professor of Global History at Oxford University, Director of the Centre for Byzantine Research and Senior Research Fellow at Worcester College. Author of *The First Crusade: The Call From The East*, and *The Silk Roads: A New History Of The World*.

Who were the main forces behind the First Crusade?
The Byzantine Empire, centred around Constantinople, was a model in managing risk - one reason it had been so stable and successful for over half a millennium after the fall of Rome. In the late 11th century, however, a build-up of pressure for multiple sources brought the empire to its knees. The Emperor Alexios I Komnenos had taken his throne by military force in a coup in 1081, and as basically a usurper with no inherited authority his position was perhaps not as stable as many of his predecessors. And the deterioration of the position in Asia Minor was serious, in particular the loss of large, fortified cities to the Turks, thereby enabling them to cement their foothold in the region. The emperor needed large-scale support to recover those - and turned to the west for expertise as well as manpower. In 1095 he sent envoys to Pope Urban II, imploring him to help fellow Christians against the scourge of the Muslim threat. The Pope did not disappoint, and at the Council of Clermont in 1095 gave a fiery and passionate speech which would ignite crusading fever.

How significant is it that the first to respond was the 'People's Crusade'?
On the back of the religious fervour drummed up in passionate campaigning by both the pope and the French cleric Peter the Hermit, the population in Western Europe had been whipped up by news of the crisis in Byzantium and beyond were responding to calls to do something about it. In military terms, however, the People's Crusade - made up of some knights but mainly ordinary devout Christians mixed together with the dispossessed, opportunists and the downright criminal and led by Peter - was totally insignificant. The People's Crusade was a disaster - chaotic, disorganised and foolhardy. A bit like a crowd of football hooligans on the rampage. It also had a very sinister and disturbing side. As this first wave of crusaders moved through Europe what could and should be done in the name of Christ was often ignored or excused away. In order to support themselves there was mass looting; in order to show their devotion to Christ there was the brutal massacre of several communities of Jews in Germany who were caught up in this fiery uncontrollable tide against all non-Christians. Such was the success, interpretation and effectiveness of the spread of the Crusade message in the mid-1090s.

Can the motives of either side be seen as purely religious?
Much depends on what one means by 'purely religious' or even by 'religious'. A lot of historians take ideas about

RIGHT
The Council of Clermont in 1095

What if...
THE FIRST CRUSADE HAD BEEN DEFEATED?

Godfrey de Bouillon was one of the leading Christian figures of the First Crusade

Boo-Hoo! I LOST!

What if... THE FIRST CRUSADE HAD BEEN DEFEATED?

THE PAST

1081-95

MILITARY PRESSURE IN THE EAST, A PERFECT STORM

The Byzantine Emperor Alexios was losing territory fast and was desperate to find some way of stopping the rot. Heavily fortified cities, that had once been his, were now being used against him by the Turks in order to bolster their advances and their ambitions as they pushed West. With the increase in pressure on his borders, despite relations between the Western and Eastern followers of Christianity being at something of a low ebb, his only option was to appeal to the West.

1095

THE REACH AND ENERGY OF THE CHURCH

Christianity permeated every corner of 11th century life in both the Byzantine Empire and Western Europe, and it was to be faith and belief that were to act as the catalyst for the forthcoming war on Islam. The rising ambitions of the papacy, and Urban II in particular, set the tone for the assistance to their fellow Christians in the East. The passion of oratory was intense, demonising the Turks through detailed, macabre and horrific descriptions of their treatment of Christians, plus the ultimate insult to Christ and Christianity – occupation by Islam of the Holy Land and Holy City of Jerusalem. With its network of priests and monks the message was carried throughout Europe, stirring up passion, anger and hatred that would call many to arms and 'follow the cross', because 'God wills it'.

1099

PILGRIMAGE

As the pinnacle of faith and devotion, it was believed that pilgrimage to the Holy Land and to Jerusalem was a cast iron guarantee of the cleansing of sins and acceptance into Heaven. The journey had always been fraught with incredible danger, but with the capture of Jerusalem, and the later establishment of the Levantine states under Christian control, such a journey of faith became more popular and more possible.

---

faith and devotion on trust – and over-rely on charter documents and other primary sources that can easily result in over-simplifications or even mislead entirely. I think motivations are always problematic as they are usually complex and their interpretation highly subjective. And, of course, they could and did change before, during and after the Crusades for participants, observers and indeed people living far away too. The initial 'call to arms' for the Crusade was, on the surface at least, very much a message of defence of the Christian faith, but the underlying issues of land, power and influence were always very close to the surface.

ABOVE The siege of Jerusalem 1099. Citizens were slaughtered after its capture

LEFT The Byzantine Emperor Alexios I Komnenos

How different could the Byzantine Empire, Western Europe and future control of the Holy Land have looked if the Crusade had been defeated? And how ambitious could the Turks potentially have been?

That's relatively easy to answer because all the Crusades effectively did was to hold up the advances of the Turks for a few hundred years. By the late 1300s the Ottomans were deep into the Balkans, bypassing Constantinople (which they finally took in 1453) and over the next five centuries occasionally threatened to overspill far beyond too. Vienna could have fallen in 1529 or in 1683.

Ironically, the more interesting question here is a counter-intuitive one: would there have been an Ottoman Empire in the first place without the Crusades? In fact, what the western expeditions to the Holy Land did was to unify the Islamic world and to paper over the very substantial political, religious and ethnic cracks to pave the way for a true Mediterranean, African and Asian superpower. I doubt that could or would have happened without the intervention of the Crusades.

What consequences would defeat have had on the reputation of the pope, the church, and the military might of Western Europe? Were other individual reputations at stake?

The Crusades were the making of Urban II and of the papacy in general. Had the expedition ended in defeat at Jerusalem in 1099, or not taken place at all, the pope would have been far less significant as a political figure in European and global history. There was a long history of competition between religious and secular leaders in the church in Western Europe; this would have continued without the Crusades, and I suspect the Pope would have got to the same place of wielding real power in the end some other way. Peter the Hermit, after heavy defeat in battle, was stopped from fleeing to the safety of Constantinople and made to suffer the same dangers and tribulations of his fellow crusaders. The prominent kings of Western Europe such as France, England and the Holy Roman Emperor took no part as, ironically, having all been excommunicated by Pope Urban II they were excluded from taking part in a 'holy war'! For the prominent nobility and military leaders, such as Raymond of Toulouse and Godfrey of Bouillon, the capture of Jerusalem was to catapult them into the realms of stardom, idealising their exploits, their honour and their heroism through heavily romanticised song and literature. The realities of anti-Semitism and the massacre of innocent men women and children after the capture and fall of the Holy City were to be ignored or conveniently forgotten. Now there was a new idealised benchmark against which levels of chivalry, honour and piety would be upheld by those crusaders who were to come, as well as firmly fixing the accepted image of the crusading knight into history for hundreds of years. Defeat of these 'heroes' would have painted a very different picture altogether.

Were there potential flaws that could have led to defeat or was victory inevitable?
This very much depends on perspective. Seen from the perspective of the capture of Jerusalem as being the sole purpose of the First Crusade then yes, it turns into a great success; but taking the Crusades as a whole they ended in failure. So, the First Crusade can be seen as a classic case of winning a battle but losing the war.

But if we are to look at the First Crusade on its own, it's a different story. It could have ended in disaster on multiple occasions. In one way, it is incredible that it did not do so, especially during the Siege of Antioch in 1098.

It should also be remembered that after travelling such a huge distance, battles and disease took a horrific toll on numbers, with only a fraction of the original armies actually making it to the walls of Jerusalem, leaving them vulnerable to larger forces and defeat or victory very much on a knife edge.

Would defeat have stopped any future Crusades in their tracks?
Defeat would have meant that an army of at least 60,000, and by some estimates and reports perhaps as many as 100,000, had failed; something of a substantial blow to the reputation of Western military might and expertise, and the stomach for any future conflict in the name of Christ or honour may have dissolved. One can also speculate that such a catastrophe would have led to a much more galvanised and even greater response - but I doubt it. It's worth remembering that Jerusalem fell to the Arabs 450 years before the Crusades, and no one made much of an effort to recover it before the 1090s, emphasising the complex and various elements that had come into play that ignited the First Crusade and then fanned the flames.

RIGHT
Godfrey de Bouillon, appointed ruler of Jerusalem but refused the title 'king'
© Getty Images

THE POSSIBILITY

LATE 11TH CENTURY

THE FALL OF BYZANTIUM'S EASTERN PROVINCES
This would have changed the nature and culture of the empire completely. The threat to their faith, trade, society and influence was already stretched to the limit. But if overwhelmed by the marauding Seljuk Turks the very fabric of the empire would have been decimated, with consequences not only for the Byzantine world, but also for Western Europe which would be denied its 'buffer zone' with Islam.

1099

THE UNION OF THE WESTERN AND EASTERN CHURCHES
Although at the time of the First Crusade relations between the Western and Eastern Christian Churches were a little cold, there was still the possibility of a stronger union on the cards. But, with the relative success of the First Crusade, the papacy saw its influence rise dramatically and so any possible strengthening of the Christian world through closer ties of East and West was derailed by the papacy's new sense of its own powers and independent ambitions.

12TH CENTURY

THE ANCHORING OF THE SELJUK STATE
The development and expansion of the Turk's territorial and cultural ambition would have come far sooner than it did. By establishing a solid foundation around Baghdad, they would have been able to look confidently both towards the West, more deeply into Europe (as they eventually did), as well as to the East and India. In addition to their eventual spread around the southern Mediterranean and North Africa this would have become a formidable Islamic empire much sooner than the West expected or was prepared for.

What if...
BRITAIN HAD NOT WON THE SEVEN YEARS' WAR?

The rise of Britain as a world power would have been severely curtailed if France had emerged victorious in this conflict

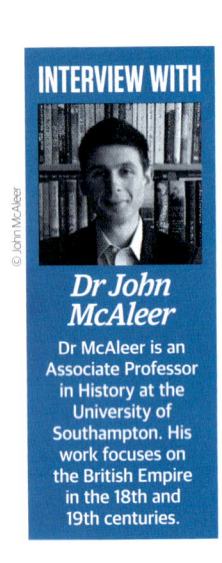

INTERVIEW WITH

Dr John McAleer

Dr McAleer is an Associate Professor in History at the University of Southampton. His work focuses on the British Empire in the 18th and 19th centuries.

What was the background to the Seven Years' War from 1756 to 1763?
In some ways, the Seven Years' War is part of a much longer war. There's 100 years of warfare between Britain and France in the 18th century, I think something like one year out of every two in the 18th century Britain and France are at war. So some historians would see the Seven Years' War as a kind of unfinished business from the previous war, the War of the Austrian Succession [1740 to 1748]. They're working out of those problems on the European continent. The second thing is a kind of ratcheting up of tension between these two emerging global superpowers. So, Britain and France going toe-to-toe around the globe looking for more trade, more commerce, more influence. That is another spark, as it were, that ignites the fire of the Seven Years' War.

Who were the major belligerents on each side of the conflict?
You've got France and Austria, quite unusually. Normally, France and Austria tend to be on opposite sides, and that suits Britain from a diplomatic perspective, the two major European powers. You've also got Spain allying herself with France. Spain doesn't enter the war until the early 1760s. So those three major powers are on one side. Then you've got Britain and Prussia on the other side.

How did the war play out?
The war between Britain and France officially breaks out in 1756, but it starts a little bit before that, actually in 1754 in the interior of North America when Britain and France are fighting out a border skirmish in the Ohio country. But

RIGHT
The Seven Years' War claimed hundreds of thousands of lives

What if...
BRITAIN HAD NOT WON THE SEVEN YEARS' WAR?

What if... BRITAIN HAD NOT WON THE SEVEN YEARS' WAR?

from the 1750s it doesn't look terribly good [for Britain]. 1757 is a terrible year for Britain; it loses Menorca; the French are on the verge of invading the south coast of England. It doesn't start off well. The turning point for many people at the time and for many historians since has been the year 1759, the so-called Year of Victories, the Year of Miracles, Annus Mirabilis. When Britain wins this series of battles in different places around the world, from West Africa to the Caribbean to India, and then ultimately [the Battle of the] Plains of Abraham outside Quebec City in North America. That turns the tide in favour of Britain. It takes another four years for peace, eventually signed in 1763. But ultimately, those victories in 1759 are the ones that had turned the tide for Britain.

With so many different theatres of war, was this essentially a world war?
Well, yes. I call the Seven Years' War the First World War. But I've got a lot of other colleagues who use the same term for lots of other wars, like the Crimean War. There are plenty of historians who work on particular wars and term them global wars. But yes, I can see this being described as a world war, and that is the mobilisation of resources on a global scale. There are battles on three, four continents.

What were the major outcomes of the war? Did it allow Britain to become a global superpower?
I think one of my favourite questions from the Seven Years' War is: did the Seven Years' War cause as many problems as opportunities for Britain? So yes, it absolutely did because there were lots of opportunities for Britain to establish herself as a global superpower. It is worth saying that Britain is a really young country when the war breaks out. It's less than 50 years old, so after the Union of the Parliament in 1707, the outbreak of the war is 49 years [later]. The Seven Years' War is one of these events that helps to forge some sort of national identity. Just as important, of course, is the trading and commercial opportunities the Seven Years' War and victory in it affords to Britain are really important. It gives Britain that opportunity to expand over the course of the next three or four decades.

What if the war hadn't swung in Britain's favour in 1759 and they had lost the war?
In some ways we need to [re-think] our 20th century approach to warfare where it's total surrender. That's not the way they did things in the 18th century. Fighting a war was basically a way of gathering credit that you then bargained off at the negotiating table. If France had won the war, it would depend on what France had captured. Which Caribbean islands would France have captured? Which bits of North America would France have captured that they would then bargain with Britain? What kind of balance of power would there have been at the end of the Seven Years' War? It would depend on how successful the French were. If they managed to invade Britain, well, then that would've been a quite different matter I guess. It would've, obviously, led to a drain on national resources and all the rest here in Britain. Some historians would say that winning the Seven Years' War wasn't all it was cracked up to be. It had increased national debt tremendously, put a lot of pressure on the East India Company in Asia, and led, ultimately, to some of the problems in the North American colonies that led to the War of American Independence.

Were there any key territories that France had its eye on?
The French are interested in Europe, principally. Obviously, they'd be keen to capture some of those really rich, sugar-producing colonies in the Caribbean if they could do that. But I think there are two different strategies at play here. There's the French strategy of trying to clear Britain out of the Mediterranean, so capturing the island of Menorca in the Western Mediterranean. But essentially, France gets forced into supporting her ally Austria and fighting the war in Europe. Whereas Britain, particularly under the prime-ministership of William Pitt the Elder,

> "The Seven Years' War is an event that helps to forge some sort of national identity"

ABOVE
The Plains of Abraham near Quebec was one of the war's key battles

focused on the wider world and winning the war by winning lots of colonies. So it's two different approaches to the war.

How would the balance of power in North America had shifted?

If France had been successful in North America, if they'd avoided Quebec being captured by the British, if they'd managed to hold onto those territories, it would've kept a screw on the British settlers in North America. It would've prevented them from expanding into the interior. It would've prevented them from settling in places like Ohio and those kind of places in the interior of North America. I think that would've been a major effect if Britain hadn't won the Seven Years' War.

Did the Seven Years' War allow the British Empire to grow into the global superpower it became?

I think it definitely played a major role in it, in some cases because of the direct effects of the war. In India, for example, because of Britain being at war with France, it gave the East India Company an opportunity to beat the French in India. In terms of capturing areas in West Africa and in terms of protecting Britain's colonies in the Caribbean, it definitely cemented that Atlantic Empire for Britain as well. By holding onto these colonies it meant that their sugar-producing, profit-making ability was retained for the Empire. Ultimately it set the ball rolling for all those upheavals in North America over the course of the next decade or two that led to the emergence of the United States. If you want to take it a step further, you might say it forced a re-imagining of the British Empire, as it were, forcing it to move away from the Atlantic and turn more towards Asia and India. So yeah, it helps to put Britain on the map as a global superpower. It also helps to put Prussia on the map as a European superpower.

Would Britain's place in the world ultimately have changed dramatically if they had lost?

It would've definitely changed Britain's place in the world and Britain's view of itself if it had lost the war. It depends on how catastrophically they would've lost the war, because Britain loses the War of American Independence but isn't particularly bothered by that because it's managed to hold on to Jamaica. Would they have lost the war catastrophically? I don't know. But as I said, Britain is a pretty young country in the 1750s and 1760s, so it definitely would've had an effect on its view of itself and its place in the world for a while to come.

LEFT
Many describe the Seven Years' War as a world war

Balance of Power

Throughout the 18th century, the major European powers of Britain, France, the Netherlands, Prussia, Austria and others would constantly vie for power and influence, often motivated by a desire to not see one nation gain too much control or hegemony over the continent. The concept of a European balance of power was a major influence on several wars in this period, with the War of the Spanish Succession, War of the Austrian Succession, the Seven Years' War, the War of the Bavarian Succession and the Napoleonic Wars all following a similar trend. Sometimes these major nations would be direct combatants, as in the Seven Years' War, and other times they would aim to aid one side against another with arms or funds. After the Seven Years' War, many European nations backed the American War of Independence to try to dent the growing power and imperial dominance of the British crown around the world.

Alliances across Europe were constantly shifting as powers rose and fell

What if...

GERMANY HAD WON WWI?

A German victory in the First World War would set them up as the de facto dominant force in Europe

INTERVIEW WITH
Stephen Badsey
Stephen Badsey is a professor of Conflict Studies at the University of Wolverhampton. An internationally recognised military historian, he has written or edited more than 120 books and articles, his writings have been translated into eight languages, and he appears frequently on television and in other media.

RIGHT
A company believed to be the Public Schools Battalion (16th Battalion), prior to the Battle of the Somme, 1916

FAR RIGHT
If Germany had won WWI against Britain then Adolf Hitler might not have become a German leader

What would have happened if Germany had won World War I?
It depends on when they win it. If they win a short war in 1914, with the Schlieffen Plan [the plan to quickly defeat the French first to avoid fighting on two fronts] working, it's different than if they win a negotiated victory after a long, hard fight at the end of 1916 or early in 1917, which is the other possibility. Either way, you get a large German Empire dominating central and Western Europe. What is likely to happen is you get a very strong and dominant Germany, [but one] that is not quite as bad as Hitler's Germany in two respects. One is that it doesn't have a plan for the genocide of the Jewish population of Europe – at least, we don't think it would have – and it doesn't have a plan for global domination. With those two exceptions, you get a very nasty, racist, expansionist state with enough power in terms of economic and political power to dominate Europe, which means it can do something no power had ever been able to do: it can afford to have an extremely large and extremely good army, and it can also afford to have an extremely good navy, large enough to defeat the Royal Navy. They don't actually have to invade Britain, although they probably would, but they can just starve it into submission.

Would this have led to another war?
If Germany wins World War I, they get into a strong position [against the rest of Europe], and then there's almost certainly a war about ten years later, in which the British are defeated. So, the British have absolutely no motive for letting this happen. In 1914, the British have three things that nobody else on the planet has got: they've got the world's only global empire with massive resources, they've got dominant control of the world's financial systems through London, and they've got the biggest and most powerful navy in the world. So, why should they sit there doing nothing while a country that will almost certainly defeat them in the next war ten years on establishes that position [to leapfrog them]?

Without a German defeat, is there any chance of someone like Hitler still rising to power?
The short answer is yes. Mussolini came to power in Italy, and Italy was on the winning side in World War I. The Treaty of Versailles was [Hitler's] excuse; no reputable historians believe that World War II leads inevitably from World War I. The idea that a botched peace treaty in 1919 inevitably leads to World War II is not historically accurate.

What might a victorious German Empire have looked like in practice?
Again, it depends on when it happens. At the start of the war in 1914, the Germans have no real concept of any war aims except reaching the enemy capital, which had been their experience in the Franco-Prussian War from 1870 to 1871, for example. When that fails in September 1914, they realise they're going to need some war aims, so they come up with something called the 'Septemberprogramm'. This is a plan for the domination of Belgium as a client state, the Netherlands, which is neutral,

What if...
GERMANY HAD WON WWI?

"What is likely to happen is you get a very strong and dominant Germany that is not quite as bad as Hitler's Germany."

What if... GERMANY HAD WON WWI?

> "We might well have seen a war against that kind of German empire [...] in a manner not too dissimilar to WWII"

the annexation of large parts of northern France with its industry, an absorption of parts of the Austro-Hungarian Empire and the establishment of a German frontier further to the East. All of this would produce a German-dominated super-state that would reach roughly from Calais to as far east as Kyiv.

Could Germany have won the war with the entrance of the United States?
As it happened, the Germans made the conscious decision instead to try to go for another total win by introducing unrestricted submarine warfare in January to February 1917 in an attempt to starve the British out, and that was the principal decision that brought the US into the war. Once the US is in the war as well, it's difficult for the Germans to come up with any kind of win; they make a last attempt with their spring offensives after the collapse of Russia in the spring of 1918, but these do not succeed.

What would a German victory in World War I have meant for the US?
A dominant Germany in Europe does not pose a direct threat to the United States, and given the physical distances involved with the Atlantic, it is entirely possible that the United States would simply accept this position. President Woodrow Wilson had been re-elected in 1916 on the basis of having kept the United States out of World War I, but when German submarines started sinking American transport ships on the high seas in early 1917, they are compelled to enter the war. So, in the short term, the United States might well have taken the view that this was no threat to it. What might then happen half a century on is an open question, but if Germany had developed into the kind of powerful, aggressive state most historians think it would, it's entirely possible it would have challenged in South and Central America, or it might have challenged in the Atlantic or the Pacific [Oceans]. We might well have seen a war against that kind of German empire, going to war with the United States in a manner not too dissimilar to World War II.

How would Britain have responded?
Even if there is a complete and spectacular German victory in 1914, which is not likely, as people have been trying to make a quick German win with the Schlieffen Plan work perfectly more or less ever since the battle actually took place. Even if that happens and France surrenders as it did in 1914, the imperative for the British to avoid the domination by any one power of Europe is so great that you would get a situation similar to that which the British faced with France under Napoleon a century earlier, that they would just keep rebuilding coalitions against this hostile Germany. And you could envisage that the British could just about mount the equivalent of D-Day, taking a British counter-invasion, either of France, Belgium or even the German coastline some time in 1916. So hypothetically you might have seen D-Day several decades before it took place.

If the US hadn't entered the war, would they still have grown into the global superpower they are today, or would they be more isolated?
The US entry into World War I established its position as an important global power. Indeed, one of the effects of World War I is that the new Soviet Union and the US emerge as non-European powers for the first time, playing a major role in the international system. And the effect of World War II is to establish the domination of those two non-European powers, the US and Soviet Union, with the European powers no longer playing the role they had played recently. This lasts through to the end of the Cold War in 1990 and 1991. Would the US have emerged into its assumption after 1945 of global interests without its involvement in World War I? I would say it's unlikely. If Germany doesn't threaten the US or its interests, you're going to see a more isolationist US. If a confident, expansionist, aggressive and militaristic Germany starts to threaten the US, the US would almost certainly respond.

Would the League of Nations and, ultimately, the United Nations still have materialised under a German victory?
No, the League of Nations was very much the ideal of President Woodrow Wilson. And, of course, the US itself doesn't join the League of Nations, but it is a product of the peace of Paris, including the Treaty of

HOW WOULD IT BE DIFFERENT?

REAL TIMELINE

1914

- **Franz Ferdinand assassinated**
  The heir to the throne of the Austro-Hungarian Empire, Franz Ferdinand, and his wife Sophie are assassinated while on a visit in Sarajevo, Bosnia.
  28 June 1914

- **Germany offers support**
  Kaiser Wilhelm II offers German support for Austria-Hungary against Serbia. This leads to Austria-Hungary ultimately declaring war on Serbia on 28 July.
  5 July 1914

- **Declaration of war**
  After Austria-Hungary declares war on Serbia, Germany in turn declares war on Russia and, two days later, also on France. After Germany invades Belgium, Britain feels forced to enter the war as well.
  1 August 1914

- **The Battle of Mons**
  The British Expeditionary Force (BEF) retreats after the Battle of Mons with the advancing German First Army making ground.
  23 August 1914

- **The Schlieffen Plan**
  Germany must decide whether to try for an immediate outright victory in Western Europe with their Schlieffen Plan, or engage in a longer war with the Allied nations.
  September 1914

ALTERNATE TIMELINE

ABOVE
WWI saw true industrial warfare for the first time in history

Versailles in 1919. What you would see is something with some kind of form in Europe, an extension of what is known as the Zollverein, the pan-German Customs Union of the 19th century, forming into something which would bear some resemblance to the modern EU but only to the extent that it would be a very large trading block. Its laws, traditions and attitudes towards human rights would have been completely different. But no, with a German victory in WWI, the League of Nations and from it at the end of World War II, the United Nations, I don't think there's any way this would happen.

Would Russia still have become the Soviet Union?
Russia had its own problems. It had already had its minor revolution, the uprisings of 1905, leading to political reforms and the creation of a Russian parliament, the Duma. If France is defeated in 1914, Russia probably makes peace with Germany and Austria-Hungary fairly quickly. What basis that will be made on is very hard to say at the moment, but it will almost certainly have been a limited Russian defeat. But what happens after that is not particularly connected with the war; it is the strain of fighting the war over the three-year period that precipitates the Russian political and economic collapse, and without that, the idea of a Russian revolution in the way it actually happened is not a certainty.

Do you think World War II would have still happened?
If you got the Germany I've described, that has been successful in World War I and has achieved this kind of domination, who is going to fight it and why? The only thing that works is looking at the British strategy before, against revolutionary and Napoleonic France, where the British kept putting together alliances, kept being defeated and just wouldn't give up until Napoleon was finally defeated, and that war lasted for a quarter of a century. So you could easily envisage the British drawing on the resources of their empire, simply refusing to accept German victory and carrying out a long and persistent war on the peripheries of Europe and around the world to prevent this domination, which could have gone on for decades. Whether Britain could have brought the US in on their side is hard to construct a scenario for, but that depends almost entirely on whether Germany tries to starve Britain into submission by cutting off its supply routes.

● **Blockade of Britain**
In an attempt to starve the British, Germany begins unrestricted submarine warfare, sinking any vessels bound for Britain.
February 1915

● **The US enters the war**
After continued sinking of vessels, the US enters the war, mobilising troops immediately, while the Great German Withdrawal takes place.
6 April 1917

● **Brest-Litovsk**
Russia agrees to a negotiated peace with Germany in the Treaty of Brest-Litovsk.
3 March 1918

● **Armistice Day**
The war comes to an end as a battered Germany signs an armistice with the Allies.
11 November 1918

● **Trench warfare**
Scrapping the Schlieffen Plan, trenches are dug along the Western Front, foreshadowing a long stalemate.
November 1914

● **Blockade of Britain**
Germany attempts to starve the British island nation through their extensive U-Boat submarine campaign.
February 1915

● **Invasion**
Germany attempts to invade Britain after annexing large parts of Western Europe.
September 1915

● **Battle of the Somme**
In the bloodiest day of fighting in British military history, 60,000 Allied soldiers are dead, wounded or missing after a disastrous battle.
1 July 1916

● **US troops arrive**
The first US troops arrive in France and the Allies begin significant advancements against the Germans.
25 June 1917

● **Spring Offensive**
The German Spring Offensive fails to break down the Allied front line.
April 1918

● **Treaty of Versailles**
The Treaty of Versailles is signed, imposing strict limitations on Germany following their defeat in the war.
28 June 1919

● **Germany attacks**
The Germans decide to go ahead with the Schlieffen Plan, planning sweeping attacks across Western Europe.
November 1914

● **France surrenders**
The French surrender to Germany, with other countries in Western Europe soon following suit, apart from Britain.
December 1914

● **Russian peace**
Russia enters into a negotiated peace with Germany before the war with Britain escalates further.
June 1915

● **D-Day**
After resisting a German invasion, Britain decides to launch a ground assault on Western Europe.
March 1916

● **No US help**
With its resources floundering, Britain makes another failed attempt to bring America into the war on their side.
1917

● **Britain loses**
Ultimately, after drawing on the resources of their entire empire, Britain loses the war, leading to a dominant Germany in Europe.
1924

What if...

STALINGRAD HAD FALLEN TO THE NAZIS?

How might a Nazi victory have broken Russian courage and changed the war on the Eastern Front?

INTERVIEW WITH

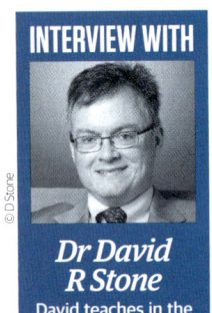

Dr David R Stone
David teaches in the Strategy and Policy Department of the US Naval War College. He received his PhD in Russian history from Yale University and is the author of numerous books and dozens of articles on Russian and Soviet military history, including *The Russian Army in the Great War: The Eastern Front, 1914-1917.*

• *These views are David's own and not any official position of the US government.*

RIGHT
Hitler's instructions were to win Stalingrad at any cost

It is a battle still celebrated today in modern Russia as the very heart and soul of their courage and fortitude against an invading army. On the surface, the Molotov-Ribbentrop non-aggression pact of 1939 between Hitler and Stalin gave each what they wanted. But Hitler wanted more. Extra land for the German people and the annihilation of the Slavs were central to his plan. All went well, until Stalingrad stood firmly in his way. The city's refusal to break came at a terrible cost in lives. But if the Nazis had managed to defeat the Soviet forces and taken the city, how might the Eastern Front, and the rest of the war, have been different?

Would the Nazis have continued their expansion eastwards and what may this have looked like?
I don't think that's likely. When the Germans got to Stalingrad in late summer 1942 and began the months-long struggle for the city, the German military was already stretched to breaking point. Keep in mind - the battle for Stalingrad was only part of a much bigger campaign. In spring and summer 1942, Hitler had sent his Wehrmacht on an offensive through eastern Ukraine and southern Russia, aiming at the Caucasus. The goal was oil: some in Chechnya but far more around Baku, in present-day Azerbaijan. Hitler's empire in Europe had very few sources of oil - basically limited to some from Romania. That wasn't nearly enough to wage the global war that Hitler was now caught up in. The oil resources of Baku were enormous. Hitler's hope was to make it to the shores of the Caspian Sea and use that oil to fuel his war.

Stalingrad ended up part of this campaign because it lay on the left flank of the German move towards the Caucasus. The Germans couldn't afford to leave Stalingrad in Soviet hands - it was a potential base of operations for the Soviets to cut off the German drive for oil. The propaganda benefit of taking the city named for Joseph Stalin was a nice bonus. But the distances involved were enormous. The German jumping-off point in spring 1942, already deep inside the Soviet Union, was 1,000 kilometres (621 miles) from Baku, and there wasn't much of a transportation network in between for the Germans to commandeer. And, of course, the Soviets made sure to wreck anything of value. As it was, the Germans had to stretch their resources very thin to make the push for Baku. While they managed to get awfully close, the eventual Soviet victory at Stalingrad forced them to withdraw in early 1943.

If the Germans HAD won at Stalingrad, it MIGHT have solved some of their resource problems. But even if that had happened, German manpower and logistics couldn't have sustained much beyond what they were trying to do in 1942. Even by late 1941, well before Stalingrad started, the German military

What if...
STALINGRAD HAD FALLEN TO THE NAZIS?

103

What if... STALINGRAD HAD FALLEN TO THE NAZIS?

THE PAST

22 JUNE 1941
RENEGING ON THE DEAL
Having used the non-aggression pact with the USSR to his own advantage, Hitler was now ready to turn the tides and push eastwards. The beginning of Operation Barbarossa saw a rapid and deadly assault from land and air deep into Soviet territory. Despite greater numbers of men and equipment, the Soviets were quickly overwhelmed and encircled, leading to the surrender of hundreds of thousands. By December 1941, despite being on the outskirts of Moscow, Barbarossa had stalled, and the Russian winter began to take its toll on the German forces.

17 JULY 1942
THE SLAUGHTER BEGINS
The assault on Stalingrad was to see some of the most ferocious, brutal, and bloody close-hand combat of the entire war. Fighting street by street, within a month the Soviet general, Vasily Chuikov, and his men were pushed into a strip along the Volga River. Stalin had refused to allow civilians to be evacuated, telling the city's defenders, "not one step back", in the belief that having their fellow Russians so closely in harm's way would prove to be the greatest motivation the Soviet troops could have. It was a huge price to pay in Soviet lives.

NOV 1942 – FEB 1943
THE TIDE TURNS
The Soviet counteroffensive aimed to turn the German's own tactics back on themselves. Instead of striking back at the Nazi forces head-on, General Georgy Zhukov sent his troops around the flanks, overwhelming Romanian forces and encircling the German lines. Now trapped, an attempt was made to breach the Soviet lines by Field Marshal Erich von Manstein, but was unsuccessful. The encircled commander of the Sixth Army, General Friedrich Paulus, creates a plan – Operation Thunderclap – but this was vetoed by Hitler, who wanted Stalingrad defended to the last. It is clear Paulus did not agree, allegedly telling his generals; "I will not shoot myself for this Bohemian Corporal", and he surrendered his forces. It has been estimated that across both sides in the Battle of Stalingrad, there were up to two million deaths and casualties.

> "The biggest effect if the Soviets lost at Stalingrad would likely have been economic loss of access to oil"

was worrying about finding enough able-bodied men. And keep in mind - there wasn't a simple way to get oil from the Caspian Sea back to Germany for fuelling the fight against the Western allies.

What would a Nazi win at Stalingrad have meant for the Russian war effort, its people, and the challenges facing the Russian leadership?
Just the fight for Stalingrad was bad enough. The city was a major industrial centre, not least for Soviet tank production. As the Germans approached Stalingrad at the end of August 1942, Hitler's Luftwaffe carried out major bombing raids that devastated the city. Once the battle for the city itself started, it got much worse. The city, with all its factories, was essentially levelled.

Perhaps an even more important issue was what the Battle of Stalingrad meant for Soviet transportation and fuel. Stalingrad sits along the western bank of the Volga River, and the Volga was - and still is - a major transportation artery. In particular, the Soviet Union in WWII didn't have much of a pipeline network, so the vast majority of the oil produced in Baku got to the rest of the Soviet Union by ship - across the Caspian Sea and then up the Volga.

Starting in summer 1942, German bombers were already dropping mines in the Volga and sinking river traffic. When the Germans reached the banks of the Volga itself, traffic was completely halted. Oil started to back up in Baku as well as on the tankers in Astrakhan. The Soviets had to turn to an alternate and much less efficient route. Oil now had to go to Guryev (now Atyrau in Kazakhstan), up the Ural River, and then by rail to the rest of the Soviet Union. The Volga was closed from summer 1942 through to April 1943, and that was even with the Soviet victory.

If the Germans had won at Stalingrad, the Volga would have been closed longer, perhaps permanently. In the best case for the Soviets, they'd be stuck for a longer time with a much less efficient delivery of oil to fuel their war. In the worst case for the Soviets, German victory at Stalingrad would have allowed them to make it all the way to Baku, and the Soviets would have lost that oil entirely. That would have put the Soviet leadership in an even tougher position and might have made them rethink whether to seek a separate peace.

Could the Germans have maintained resources for two active fronts?
By this point, Germany was already badly stretched. Winning at Stalingrad, though, would actually have eased Germany's problems a bit. Taking Stalingrad would let the Germans put part of the front line on the Volga River, which would have made for a more defensible position. Taking Stalingrad would also have made it more likely that Hitler would have been able to reach the oil fields of Baku on the Caspian Sea, which would have solved one of his resource problems.

What impact would such a victory have on morale of the German people and how might the Nazi propaganda machine have benefitted from it?
No doubt Joseph Goebbels' propaganda machine would have made a great deal out of the capture of Stalingrad - the city of Stalin. But morale was not a problem for Hitler's regime. There was no significant internal resistance at this point. That only came later, when the war was clearly lost. And German soldiers fought even harder when the war turned against Germany. There was a pretty good sense among German soldiers and civilians of what Soviet victory and Soviet occupation would mean for Germans, after all the horrific crimes they had committed against the Soviet people.

The real question was how Hitler was going to compensate for the enormous material and manpower advantages of the Allies, not whether he could get his people to actually fight.

How might the Western Allies have viewed such a victory by the Nazis and what action would they need to have taken?

It certainly would have been a major morale blow, which would partially offset the Allied successes at El Alamein and the Torch landings in North Africa. But it's hard to see much changing in terms of what the Western Allies were doing – they were already shipping raw materials and munitions to the Soviet Union. It would have shifted the route: the Persian Corridor through Iran would have been forced to detour by the Nazi capture of Stalingrad, so more aid would have had to come through other routes.

Could a German victory at Stalingrad have changed the timing of the war, and even the outcome?

Certainly, winning at Stalingrad would have staved off German defeat for a time. The Soviet victory at Stalingrad not only destroyed the entire German Sixth Army, but it was followed by an offensive that liberated huge amounts of Soviet territory (and a young Mikhail Gorbachev, who lived for a time under German occupation) and forced the Germans to rapidly evacuate their troops pushing towards Baku. It gave renewed conviction to the Soviets and to the Western Allies that the Germans could indeed be beaten.

The question of changing the outcome of the war is much tougher. One of the aspects of the history of the war that is still quite mysterious is the extent of Nazi-Soviet discussions of a potential peace deal. There's reasonably good evidence that Stalin made some kind of approach to Hitler about a separate peace, though we know almost nothing about the details. If the Soviets had been defeated at Stalingrad, and if Soviet victory seemed distant or even impossible, then Stalin might have been willing to offer Hitler substantial concessions in terms of territory or resources in order to get out of the war. That would have allowed Hitler to focus exclusively on the Western Front. While this almost certainly wouldn't have been enough to enable him to defeat the United States and the United Kingdom, it might have been enough to drag the war out even longer and force the Western Allies to accept a peace of exhaustion, leaving Hitler in power in Germany with at least some of Germany's conquests. After all, Stalingrad took place a full year and a half before the Western Allies went ashore in Normandy – imagine what D-Day would have looked like with the bulk of the German military waiting in Western Europe. US Army Chief of Staff George Marshall said that he expected the American people would be willing to fight for four years before they would get tired of the war. As it was, the US only had to fight for three and a half.

ABOVE
Many of the prisoners of war would not survive their captivity

THE POSSIBILITY

1942

NON-AGGRESSION PART 2

It is possible Stalin may have looked to turn defeat into a victory of his own. Vital Nazi resources were being exhausted on the Eastern Front, but if that problem were to go away, by Stalin offering a peace deal and cessation of combat, those resources could be used more effectively in the West against the Allies. Hitler could possibly get the land he wanted for his Lebensraum (living space) for the German people, which had been at the heart of Operation Barbarossa. And Stalin would have the breathing space to rebuild the Soviet economy and armed forces in peace, ready for any possible future conflict with the West.

JUNE 1944

D FOR DISASTER DAY

Without the distraction and drain of conflict in the East, Nazi forces would have ample opportunity to strengthen, reinforce, and regroup in the West. With such a change in strength of Nazi defences, the timing and execution of the Allied invasion of Europe may have come under close scrutiny. It may be that more than one direct route back onto the Continent would be required, perhaps from the south, in order to gain a foothold. Potentially, larger numbers of Nazi forces would have made a beach invasion more of a gamble. And even once a foothold had been created, the sheer scale of Nazi defences could have drastically slowed, or stalled, the advance across Europe towards Berlin, leading to a possible stalemate.

1945 ONWARDS

THE FOURTH REICH

With a greater depth of force between him and the invading Allies, Hitler's options may have been very different. Allied war fatigue and slow progress, plus a quiet and unpredictable Soviet Union, may have played into Hitler's hands to broker a form of peace. Germany remains intact, with him as leader and buffer between capitalist West and Communist East. So, no race to Berlin between the Soviets and the West; no East and West Berlin, no East Germany; and a very different look to the plans for a closer post-war European union.

What if...

THE PERSIANS HAD CONQUERED THE GREEKS?

A victory for the Persian Empire would establish its supremacy in the region and end the democratic experiments of Athens and others

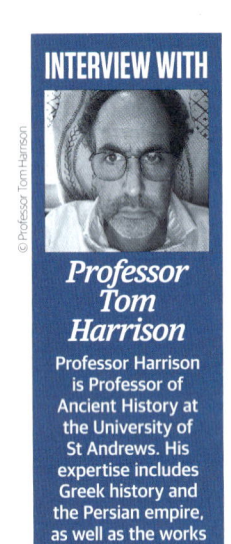

INTERVIEW WITH

Professor Tom Harrison

Professor Harrison is Professor of Ancient History at the University of St Andrews. His expertise includes Greek history and the Persian empire, as well as the works of Herodotus.

What were the Persian Wars?
The Persian Empire was the dominant political and military force in the period, and the Greeks were effectively small bit players in the whole drama. And [the Persian Wars] came about in a slightly messy way because the Greeks had participated in a revolt [in Asia Minor, the west coast of Turkey] in 499 BCE for five years. The reason why the Persian Wars were launched was effectively to kind of squash that. Athens had taken part in that revolt: they'd been asked for help and they'd sent a pathetic, measly 20 ships, and one other city had sent five ships, and they joined in the revolt. And that triggered the Persian king to seek his revenge. Herodotus [a famed Greek history writer from the time] describes those 20 ships as the beginning of evils for Greeks and Barbarians and sees that as the kind of trigger. That's the reason why a few years later they launched the campaign that led to the Battle of Marathon [in 490 BCE], which was the first wave of the Persian Wars. Then the Athenians and a few others beat the Persians at the Battle of Marathon, and then that leads to a bigger expedition around ten years later.

How did the wars play out?
It happened effectively in two kind-of rushes. One climaxes in 490 BCE, at the Battle of Marathon, which is a relatively small affair. When [the wars began again], it clearly was a much bigger deal and that was the campaign that climaxes in 480 BCE and 479 BCE, and usually people see that as the end of the Persian Wars. That's the campaign that leads to the Battle of Thermopylae, the Battle of Salamis, the Battle of Plataea and others. It kind of rumbles on though. It doesn't exactly stop. They get beaten, the Persians, and they retreat into Asia, but there are still subsequent military conflicts with them. And then the Persians go on being really a huge offstage presence in Greek history right down to Alexander the Great. So it rumbles on, but the Persian Wars really run from 490 BCE to 479 BCE.

What were the major outcomes of the Persian Wars?
For the Persian Empire, the limits of the Empire are fixed in the Mediterranean. It's clear that they wanted to have some kind of rule over Greece, possibly distant. But they probably wanted to have some control over the Mediterranean and Aegean and make sure their trade was not

RIGHT
The Battle of Marathon was a major victory for the Greeks over Persia

What if...
THE PERSIANS HAD CONQUERED THE GREEKS?

What if... THE PERSIANS HAD CONQUERED THE GREEKS?

> "The Persian Empire saw itself as a kind of global policeman that establishes peace"

interrupted by, as they would have seen it, pirates. So there was a kind of new peace, if you like, but it certainly involved them retreating back to Asia.

On the Greek side, most people have seen it as leading to a great flowering in Greek culture, a feeling of confidence, and so people for hundreds of years have seen the Greek victory in the Persian Wars as being crucial for [this].

I think the main clear outcome is that Athens develops a kind of empire. It's usually called the Athenian Empire, that lasts through the 5th century, which grows out of the alliance that they had against the Persians. It then becomes a navally based empire: lots of islands in the Aegean and eastern Mediterranean, lots of cities on the west coast of Turkey under Athens' increasingly tyrannical control. So they get lots of money from that, and a lot of the cultural flowering comes from that position of dominance that they have in the 5th century.

Was there a turning point where the Persians could have won?

Herodotus sees a moment before the Battle of Salamis [in 480 BCE] as being crucial. Because [the Athenians] stood firm, Athens survived and the Greek world survived and beat the Persians. If the Athenians hadn't stood up to the Persians, they would've ended up being divided and being beaten by the Persians. But because they won, that was the critical moment. That's, I think, the main turning point.

What if the Persians had won the Battle of Salamis and had gone on to win the Persian Wars?

For some people, if the Greeks had lost and the Persians had won, it would have been the end of Greek civilization entirely. There would have been no kind of cultural Renaissance, there would have been no democracy, and all the things for which the Ancient Greek world is looked back to as a kind of origin point wouldn't have come to pass. That's a very common view. [But] I think if it played out differently, if that whole myth hadn't developed and we could look back to a Persian Empire that had actually encouraged culture more widely in Greece and the Mediterranean, then maybe we would have a less fractured view of the world. One where there was that imagined timeless divide between East and West.

What were Persia's plans for the West if they had won?

I think there would have been winners and losers depending on exactly what happened. If Athens had held out until the end and then been defeated, then they clearly might have suffered the fate that some other cities faced, which was being basically burnt down and the men and women being sold into slavery. So it could have been virtually the end of Athens if that had been the case.

On the other hand, in the course of the Persian Wars, the Persians are making an offer to the Athenians, which is to come over and rule Greece with them and to join the Persians in alliance. They briefly contemplate that, and if they had taken up that offer and been one of the dominant places in Greece, they might've had an empire and they might've been allowed similar positions to the position they had in the 5th century. Basically, the Persians were backing whoever backed them. So if a city jumped onto their side during the Persian Wars, they were promised things. And conversely, if they held out, they were threatened with a terrible fate if they carried on resisting.

ABOVE LEFT
Some believe much of Ancient Greece owes its success to the Persian defeat

ABOVE RIGHT
Battles at Thermopylae and Salamis held Persia at bay in 480 BCE

OPPOSITE TOP
Greek Spartans fought the Persians in the Persian Wars

What exactly was the 'Greek experiment' and would that have been threatened?
The Greek experiment is a way of expressing the fact that Greek culture generated so much creativity in terms of art, literature, architecture and so on, and it generated democracies on the scale that it did. Not all Greek cities were democratic, but Athens and a number of other leading cities were. This is what that phrase 'Greek experiment' conjures up. People have imagined that the two things are linked, that there's a kind of direct link between political organisation on the one hand and culture on the other.

What would a Persian Greece have looked like?
Imagine a mosaic of control where some cities and rulers are sponsored, and there were a number of cities that had good relationships with Persia. Then I think they would've been left largely to themselves. Lots of cities in the Greek world weren't functionally independent anyway under the Athenian Empire. Tiny cities with 300 citizens weren't able to have much of a foreign policy. They had to keep their heads down and hope for the best. If one city or another would have stood up to the Persian Empire, as the Macedonians did, it is possible that there would have been a similar kind of attack on the heart of the Persian Empire in due course.

Do you think a Persian victory would have been worse for the world than a Greek victory?
No, I don't. What Athens did to its subject cities wasn't very pretty in the way in which they exercised their dominance, so people rebelled against this. It wasn't that different to the way in which the Persian Empire behaved. The Persian Empire saw itself as establishing a kind of peace in which people could get on without squabbling and without violence. So they see themselves very directly as being like a kind of global policeman who stops squabbling peoples and establishes peace.

And if you're inside the tent then you're looked after, if you're outside, you're in outer darkness. I think it's possible to glimpse a way in which Greeks might have seen the Persian Empire as an idealistic thing for the Greeks to be within, because the Greeks were endlessly squabbling. They were almost always at war with their neighbours and there might have been a chance for a more peaceful period in the aftermath of the Persian victory. The Persian Empire was in many ways no worse than any other empire.

How did the Persian Empire work?

The Achaemenid Empire was vast and varied, and as a result of that its rulers needed to be creative and flexible (up to a point) with how they controlled the provinces. Under Darius the Great the empire was divided up into provinces run by satraps. These local officials would raise taxes to fund the empire as well as maintaining local order.

In expanding the empire the Persians would also allow local leaders to remain in control and rule more or less as they had before, except now swearing fealty to the empire. This is likely how Darius would have sought to deal with Athens, which was a powerful and influential city in the region, subsuming its ideas and leadership into the mechanisms of the Achaemenid Empire. It's a model that proved to be equally effective for other empires in the years that followed, such as the Roman Empire.

Darius centralised his empire and made it follow more uniform rules

What if...

US FORCES HAD RETREATED FROM KOREA?

A victory for North Korea could have seen a humiliated America move more strongly against communism around the world

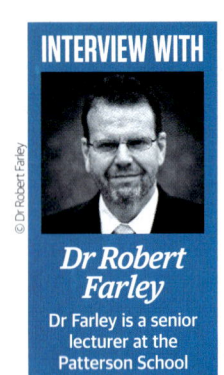

INTERVIEW WITH

Dr Robert Farley

Dr Farley is a senior lecturer at the Patterson School of Diplomacy and International Commerce at the University of Kentucky. His research and books cover military world history and politics.

What were the circumstances leading up to the Korean War?
The division of Korea happened in late 1945 after the Japanese surrender [in World War II]. The northern half of Korea was assigned to the Soviets, and the southern half was assigned to the United States. There were nationalists, Korean nationalists, on both sides. On the northern half, these were based around a guerrilla leader named Kim Il-sung. On the southern half there were a variety of leaders, but eventually they sort of coalesced around a guy named Syngman Rhee. Things were pretty violent from the beginning. A lot of people talk about the Korean War breaking out in June of 1950 as a real surprise, but there had been sporadic fighting all the way up until 1950. What happened in June was that the North Koreans launched a much more significant offensive into the South, with the approval of the Soviet Union, although not its direct support. That offensive was wildly successful and threatened to just roll up the entire peninsula.

How did the war play out?
The United States decided to intervene almost immediately. It deployed troops and aircraft and warships to the area. The troops were known as Task Force Smith, [but] were not well prepared to fight the North Koreans. They didn't have the right kind of equipment, they didn't have modern training, and so they were pushed back along with the Republic of Korea, the South Korean troops. For the first few months of the war, the North Koreans took Seoul, [and] they rolled down the peninsula. But the Americans and the South Koreans were able to establish a perimeter at a place called Pusan. They were able to protect that perimeter with lots of air support and with lots of naval support, despite several massive North Korean offensives. Essentially, they were trying to break things open.

What happened next?
So the Americans decided to intervene with a lot more force. And General Douglas MacArthur, with the support of the United Nations, launches an amphibious invasion of the Korean Peninsula at Incheon, which is half way up the peninsula off the west coast of Korea. That sort of undercut the entire North Korean offensive, and the North Koreans retreated rapidly up the peninsula. [Eventually it finishes] at the 38th parallel in 1953.

RIGHT
The Korean War claimed hundreds of thousands of lives

Could Pusan have been a turning point where America could have lost the war?
Yeah, I think so. If [North Korea] had punched through that perimeter that would have been the end of the war. It's unlikely that the US would have gone through with the amphibious invasion of the coast at Incheon. Essentially the entire Republic of Korea would have been occupied and in exile if Pusan had fallen.

What would have been the major implications of America losing?
I think that just how the US reacted to other reversals during the Cold War, we would have doubled down on a number of other areas in which we were in conflict with the Soviet Union. I think it probably would have gone badly for [Fidel] Castro in Cuba. I doubt that anyone would have been willing to allow the establishment of a Communist regime in Cuba. I think we'd have had a much more substantial commitment to Vietnam to prevent what happened in Korea. There would probably be some other places where you would have seen a heavier US involvement.

How would this have affected presidential elections in the US?
The Korean War happens at the same time as the 'Red Scare' in the United States. Essentially the source of the Red Scare is this idea that the US gave away China to the Communists, that we didn't support the Chinese government heavily enough. Eisenhower is a relative moderate on these questions. He believed that McCarthy was a buffoon and a number of other things. And so the United States, [after] losing

What if...
US FORCES HAD RETREATED FROM KOREA?

What if... US FORCES HAD RETREATED FROM KOREA?

China, then losing Korea, you might get a substantially more radical Republican candidate in 1952. I'm not sure it would be McCarthy, who had all sorts of problems. But there were other anti-Communist candidates who were more aggressively anti-Communist than Eisenhower was. And if one of those were elected in 1952 then that has a series of follow-on effects. Potentially the reaction to the 1956 revolution in Hungary becomes an interesting question. And so yeah, you might see domestic politics in the United States is uglier and more anti-Communist as a result of losing Korea.

Do you think a unified Korea would have been able to thrive?
There's almost no reason to believe that a unified Korea under Pyongyang would be as prosperous or as democratic as [South] Korea is today. In 1950, North Korea was the industrialized part. Even in 1953 after all the bombing, North Korea was more industrialised and more economically productive than South Korea. But the Kim regime has really run the economy of North Korea into the ground. The Japanese left [South] Korea in a fairly advanced state, although the Koreans will absolutely reject that if you tell them that is the case, but it's true.

Who would a unified Korea have allied with?
They might have been a little less dependent on [China and the Soviet Union], but they would have faced a very difficult set of choices about how to navigate between Beijing and Moscow in the 1960s. I think it's really hard to imagine them doing anything really innovative like trying to break away from both communist superpowers and some sort of move towards the United States. And so I think the foreign policy would probably in a lot of ways be similar to what we actually saw from North Korea.

Do you see any scenario where a unified communist Korea becomes a major player in the spread of communism around the world?
North Korea, even as it was, sent weapons and advisors to a lot of places around the developing world, especially Latin America and so forth and so actively undertook steps to try to spread socialist revolution. It never really worked out, but still North Korean weapons were everywhere. It seems likely that Pyongyang would have done that anyway, but I'm not sure it would have been any more successful than it was in the real world. Had the US

ABOVE
President Eisenhower may have struggled for election in 1952 had America lost

RIGHT
An armistice was signed in 1953

LEFT
A political cartoon depicting the devil painting Washington red

BELOW
Kim Jong-un is North Korea's leader today

> "The Korean War happens at the same time as the 'Red Scare' in the United States"

lost the Korean War, they would have doubled down on anti-Communism almost everywhere and would have pushed back even harder.

If America had lost, would North Korea have picked another enemy like Japan to focus on?
A lot of the rhetoric and propaganda that comes out of the Kim regime today is directed against the Japanese rather than the South Koreans. I think the problem is that if North Korea is not communist and weird and paranoid, then it has no reason to exist, because South Korea is such a successful example of a capitalist democratic country. And you take that example away and the behaviour might be different.

Would the North Koreans still have developed nuclear weapons?
I think it's very possible that the North Koreans might have decided to go ahead and develop nuclear weapons anyway. I mean, it would have been a large industrial economy with lots of human capital, with lots of know-how. They would have been one of the most thriving economies in the Soviet bloc, certainly larger even than East Germany, and so probably would have been the third largest economy in the entire Soviet bloc after the Soviet Union and China.

Is the world a better place because North Korea didn't win?
I think it's impossible to say. However, there are 33 million people in South Korea, and their lives are incontrovertibly better today than they would be if North Korea had won the war. That wasn't even really the reason we fought it, but South Korea is a thriving democratic market-oriented economy, and there's almost no way to imagine that those outcomes would have happened if North Korea had won the war. Now the war caused a lot more misery for the people of North Korea, but South Korea is a frontline democracy and a part of the family of nations. And I don't see the Kim regime having ever been able to do that.

Domino Theory

"You have a row of dominoes set up, you knock over the first one, and what will happen to the last one is the certainty that it will go over very quickly. So you could have a beginning of a disintegration that would have the most profound influences." Such was President Eisenhower's explanation of Domino Theory in 1954, the predominant foreign policy theory of the United States from the 1950s to the 1980s. The concern was that if the US allowed Southeast Asian nations to 'succumb to communism' without challenge then another and another would fall as a result, wiping out Western democratic influence. It was believed that the US had already allowed China to adopt communist rule too easily, which is why it engaged in conflict in both the Korean peninsula and Vietnam in the years that followed.

Eisenhower's concern over the spread of communism may well have been linked to fears about the proliferation of atomic weapons

What if...
NAPOLEON HAD WON THE BATTLE OF WATERLOO?

Would a loss still have been inevitable even if Napoleon had defeated the British at Waterloo?

INTERVIEW WITH
Alan Forrest
Alan Forrest is emeritus professor of modern history at the University of York. He has written widely on French revolutionary and Napoleonic history. His books include *Napoleon's Men: The Soldiers Of The Revolution And Empire*, and a biography simply called *Napoleon*. He also wrote a book on the Battle of Waterloo for Oxford University Publishing's Great Battles series, released for the battle's bicentenary in 2015.

Mark Adkin
Mark Adkin is a military historian who took up writing after serving in the British Army for 18 years and over ten years in the Colonial Service in the Pacific. He is the author of *The Waterloo Companion: The Complete Guide To World's Most Famous Land Battle*, *The Western Front Companion*, and *The Sharpe Companion*, which placed Bernard Cornwell's Sharpe novels in historical content.

RIGHT
Napoleon is beaten in battle at the Battle of Leipzig

What would have happened if Napoleon had won the Battle of Waterloo?
Alan Forrest: He would certainly have taken Brussels and he might have tried to advance toward the boundary of the Rhine and Schelt. But there was no possibility of long-term success. He would surely have gone on to lose within weeks or months, because although the British, Dutch, Belgians and Prussians were involved at Waterloo, neither the Austrians nor the Russians were, and they had armies of 150,000 to 200,000 waiting in the wings. In particular, the Tsar wanted Napoleon destroyed: he didn't believe Europe could remain at peace if Napoleon remained at large.
Mark Adkin: I wouldn't have thought [that Napoleon would have enjoyed success for] more than a few weeks. If he had won the battle, Wellington would have withdrawn what was left of his army and Napoleon would have had to hurry back to Paris. The Allies would have waited until the Austrians and Russians had arrived and the British and Prussians had recovered, then would have teamed up together. Napoleon wouldn't have had much chance at all.

Why did Napoleon lose at Waterloo?
Adkin: Napoleon had a big problem because he was surrounded by various countries that were desperate to get rid of him. There were four main threats once he established himself back in Paris: The Anglo-Dutch Army under Wellington in Belgium, the Prussians under Blücher in Germany, the Russians under Barclay De Tolly, and the Austrians under Schwarzenberg. That's nearly half million men under arms and they all planned to converge on Paris. The only way he could possibly win was to make the maximum use of the time it was going to take Russians and the Austrians and so on to get there. While they were marching, he had to deal with the others, in particular Wellington and Blücher. He wanted to defeat the Prussians at Ligny, while Wellington was held off by a smaller force. Once the Prussians were defeated, he could turn the combined strength on Wellington. He succeeded partially at Ligny - his strategy worked and he split the two Allies, turned on the Prussians and defeated them, but he didn't crush them. He let them withdraw and recover. That was a mistake. Napoleon allowed them to withdraw north instead of east, and by withdrawing north they were able to turn and then rejoin Wellington's forces.

Forrest: Napoleon had no possibility of finding large numbers of additional soldiers because he was now reliant on the French population alone, and while he was on Elba, France had abolished conscription. As long as the Allies could unite their forces against him, he was hopelessly outnumbered, and his failure to drive home his advantage after Ligny proved to be a fatal mistake.

So if Napoleon had stopped the Prussians at Ligny, he would have defeated the British at Waterloo?
Adkin: Wellington knew the Prussians were coming; he had been promised that they were coming, which is the actual reason why he stood at Waterloo and defended that bridge. If he knew the Prussians were not coming, then he would probably have withdrawn until he could join the Prussians and therefore the battle would not have taken place, not there anyway. So the crucial thing is the Prussians and their arrival clinched it [the battle].

Did the people of France support Napoleon's return from Elba?
Forrest: The most important thing to remember is that the French people were war-weary in 1815; they wanted peace above all else and few believed Napoleon could deliver that. On the other hand, there was no enthusiasm for the Bourbons and certainly no desire to go back to the Ancién Regime. The fear was that the Bourbons would try to restore the kind of aristocratic and clerical authority that had existed previously. Napoleon had surrounded himself with luxury and riches

What if...
NAPOLEON HAD WON THE BATTLE OF WATERLOO?

"They had to be sure France would be a responsible member of the international community. They had to get rid of Napoleon"

What if... NAPOLEON HAD WON THE BATTLE OF WATERLOO?

THE ARMIES AT WATERLOO

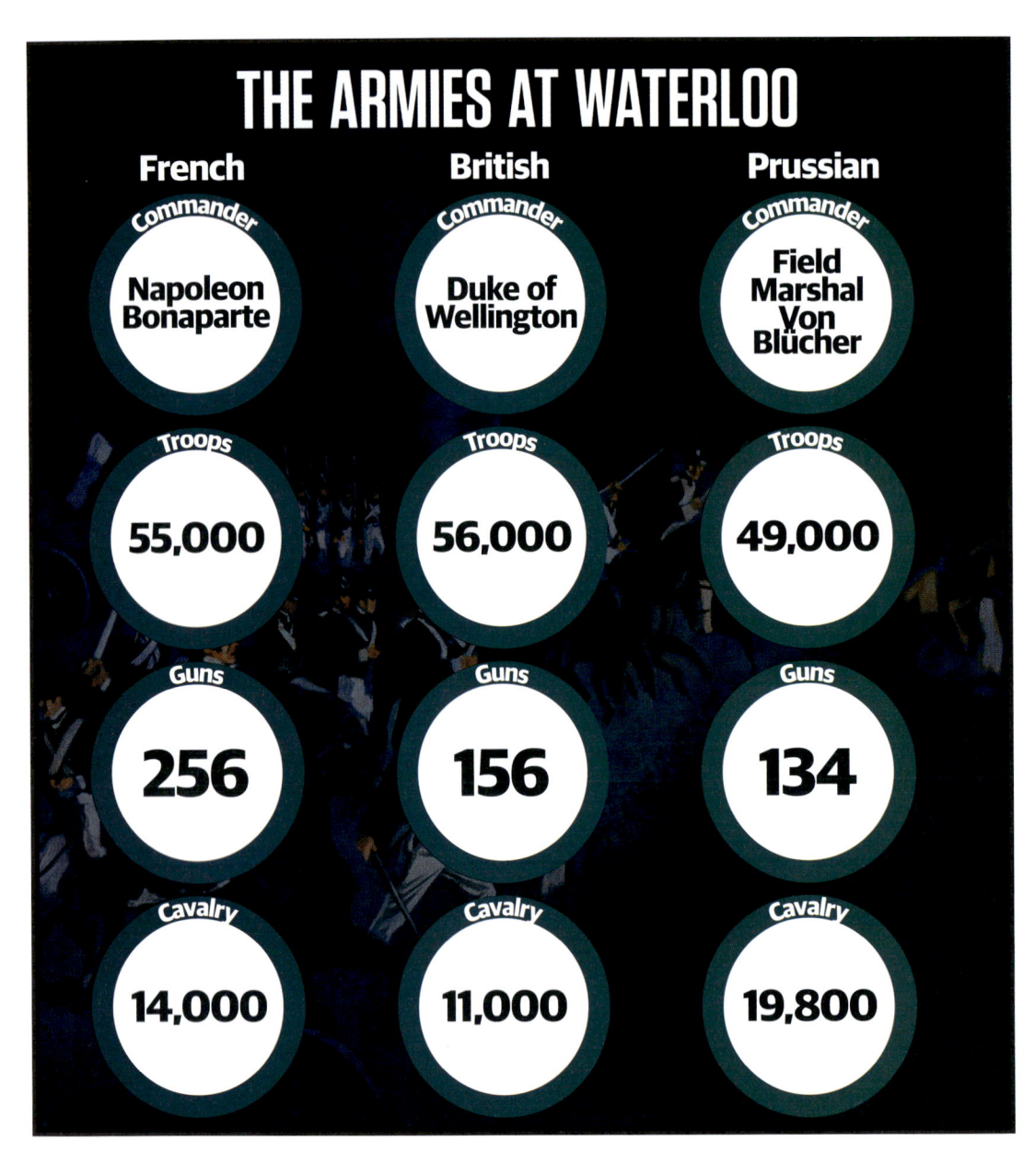

	French	British	Prussian
Commander	Napoleon Bonaparte	Duke of Wellington	Field Marshal Von Blücher
Troops	55,000	56,000	49,000
Guns	256	156	134
Cavalry	14,000	11,000	19,800

at the height of the empire, but when he returned from Elba in 1815 he sought to present himself as the little corporal of the army who had risen through talent to be its commander, but who remained essentially a man of the people, true to the ideals of the Revolution of 1789. This proved a clever tactic.

Adkin: Most of the old soldiers were tremendously loyal to Napoleon. Napoleon had raised the standing of the ordinary French soldier during all those campaigns. He was extremely generous and gave them good pay. When he came back from Elba, I think thousands of these men, who had been thrown out of the army by the Bourbons coming back, had nothing and were no longer the number-one citizens like they used to be, so they rejoined Napoleon in their thousands.

If he abandoned his imperial ambitions, could Napoleon have negotiated to stay in power in France rather than the Allies restoring the Bourbons again?

Adkin: He tried to at the beginning, after escaping from Elba. He tried then to convince the European powers he wanted to avoid war and that he renounced all claims to Belgium, Holland, Germany and Poland. He was unsuccessful, of course.

Forrest: This was never realistic. Russia wouldn't allow it and I'm not sure that Britain would, either. Britain did, however, want France to remain a viable European power since it was an important part of the balance of power structure on which peace depended. Britain was aware of the possibility of a rampant nationalistic Prussia and was very aware of the threat

HOW WOULD IT BE DIFFERENT?

REAL TIMELINE

- **Battle of Leipzig**
  Napoleon is decisively beaten in battle for the first time, by a coalition including troops from Russia, Prussia, Austria and Sweden. He is forced to return to France but the coalition continues to pursue him.
  16 October 1813

- **Napoleon abdicates**
  After being defeated by the Allies of the Sixth Coalition, Napoleon is exiled to the island of Elba. The pre-revolutionary Bourbon monarchy is restored and Louis XVIII becomes King of France.
  11 April 1814

- **Beginning of Napoleon's Hundred Days**
  Napoleon escapes Elba and after landing on the French mainland convinces the regiment sent to incept him to join him and march on Paris. As he moves north, more soldiers defect to join him. King Louis XVIII flees to the Netherlands.
  26 February 1815

- **Congress of Vienna**
  Representatives of Austria, Britain, France, Russia, and Prussia declare Napoleon an 'outlaw', marking the beginning of the War of the Seventh Coalition.
  13 March 1815

- **The Waterloo Campaign**
  Napoleon battles the Prussians at Ligny as marshal Michel Ney and Wellington fight the inconclusive Battle of Quatre Bras. The battle with the Prussians was vital as if Napoleon won he could concentrate on the British.
  16-18 June 1815

ALTERNATE TIMELINE

- **Napoleon defeats Wellington**
  After defeating the Prussians, Napoleon waits for the battleground to dry before manoeuvring artillery and cavalry to attack the Anglo-Army at Waterloo. Facing substantial loss of life, Wellington retreats to the British garrison in Brussels.
  18-19 June 1815

posed by Russia, especially in the Balkans and the eastern Mediterranean. Britain particularly needed to maintain lines of communication with India. Remember that Britain was an emerging global power in 1815 and that the Russians were aware of that. So they needed to protect France's position, but that also meant that they had to be sure France would be a responsible member of the international community. For that reason they had to get rid of Napoleon. It didn't really matter who else was there, the Bourbons would do, but they were sure that they did not want Napoleon to play that role.

If they wouldn't accept him as a ruler of France, would the Allies have still exiled him to St Helena and risked him escaping again?
Forrest: Napoleon himself was much more terrified after Waterloo of falling into the hands of the Bourbons, who might have done just that. He chose to surrender to the English in the hope that he would be allowed to live as a prisoner under house arrest in England; in other words, the British would treat him decently, with a modicum of respect. As we know, the British rejected that option and exiled him to St Helena, a remote island in the South Atlantic, far removed from Europe, from which there was little possibility he could escape. In France he could have faced a trial for treason and possible execution, as happened with Michel Ney and others of Napoleon's loyal lieutenants. But that course was not without its dangers. The regime would have risked turning Napoleon into a political martyr and, given the devotion in which he was held by his followers, it surely would have got one. I think you could make the point that the Allies had to deal with Napoleon a little delicately in 1815, because there was a real danger that they would create a martyr, in the process dividing French opinion and risking lasting instability.

If France did destabilise and wasn't able to balance power in Europe, how would this change history?
Forrest: Britain becomes the dominant world power of the 19th century, which is what did happen anyway. The next challenge, except for the colonial wars in China and so on, is going to be the Crimean War, which essentially means the balance of power that was established with events in 1815 more or less holds.

ABOVE
Napoleon was exiled to the Italian island of Elba but returned to Paris and declared himself emperor

- **Wellington defeats Napoleon**
  Napoleon attempts to wipe out Wellington's centre troops with attacks before the Prussians arrive. However, he engages too late after waiting for the ground to dry and Blücher arrives. Napoleon retreats.
  19 June 1815

- **Paris turns on Napoleon**
  Napoleon returns to the capital in defeat three days after Waterloo to find the public no longer support national resistance. While his brother Lucien believes he can still seize power by dissolving the parliament, Napoleon senses the change and abdicates his throne in favour of his son.
  22 June 1815

- **Napoleon sent to St Helena**
  Napoleon is banished to the remote island of St Helena without any of the perks he enjoyed on Elba. He dies of natural causes in 1821.
  23 October 1815

- **Michel Ney executed**
  Napoleon's long-time ally and marshal at the Battle of Waterloo, Michel Ney is executed as a warning to Napoleon's supporters.
  7 December 1815

- **Austro-Russian invasion**
  The Austrian and Russian armies combined siege of Paris overwhelms the French, with Barclay de Tolly drawing on his experiences of capturing the city in 1814.
  July 1815

- **Hundred Days ends**
  After the president of the provisional government intimates he should leave Paris, Napoleon exits the capital. Soon after Graf von Zieten's Prussian I Corps enters Paris and defeat the French. Louis XIII is restored.
  8 July 1815

- **Napoleon surrenders**
  After the British Navy blocks his attempt to take a ship to America, Napoleon surrenders himself to Captain Frederick Maitland of HMS Bellerophon and is transported to England.
  15 July 1815

- **Emperor again**
  Returning triumphant to Paris Napoleon is unopposed as he dissolves parliament and assumes dictatorial powers to better defend Paris from attack.
  21 June 1815

- **Napoleon executed**
  After his surrender the Allies allow Louis XVIII to execute Napoleon as they believe he is a threat to Europe's peace. However, the move divides France and Napoleon becomes a martyr.
  July 1815

- **The Bonaparte Spring**
  Bonapartists inspired by Napoleon's promises of constitutional reform during his Hundred Days are outraged at his execution and protest against Bourbon rule in Paris.
  15 July 1815

- **Outbreak of civil war**
  Disillusioned Napoleonic generals and officials seize on pro-Bonaparte feeling amongst the masses to make a grab for power. Events escalate and civil war erupts across France.
  September 1815

- **Rise of the British Empire**
  Britain seizes abandoned French colonies and with a self-destructing France unable to balance European power, the Crimean War between Britain and Russia is possibly hastened.
  Mid-19th century

What if...

BRITAIN HAD WON THE WAR OF INDEPENDENCE?

If Britain had won the American War of Independence, what would the greater impact have been?

INTERVIEW WITH
Prof Stephen Conway
Stephen Conway is a professor of history at University College London. His teaching focuses on 18th-century British and colonial American history and his publications include *The British Isles And The War Of American Independence* (2000) and *A Short History Of The American Revolutionary War* (2013).

Prof Emeritus John Ferling
A specialist in early American history, John Ferling has written books such as *Struggle For A Continent: The Wars Of Early America* (1993) and *Almost A Miracle: The American Victory In The War Of Independence* (2007).

Prof Robert Allison
Robert Allison has taught American history at Suffolk University in Boston, MA, since 1992, when he earned his doctorate in the History of American Civilisation at Harvard University. He chairs Suffolk's History department and teaches history at the Harvard Extension School. His books include *The American Revolution: A Concise History* (2011) and *The Boston Tea Party* (2007).

What if Britain had won the American War of Independence?
Stephen Conway: The American colonies would have remained in the British Empire, at least for the time being. Perhaps the colonies would have reconciled themselves to a restoration of British control and gradually moved towards greater home rule and eventual independence in the same manner as many countries in the later British Commonwealth. But it's equally likely that the rebellion might have flared up again in a few years, or the British government might have thought it was too expensive to maintain a large army of occupation in the conquered colonies and de facto independence would have been granted.

Is it likely that victory for Britain would have merely delayed American independence? Or could the USA still be part of the Commonwealth today?
Robert Allison: Either one is possible. [Benjamin] Franklin thought that independence would come naturally; he anticipated something like the British Commonwealth. He thought it would be impossible, when the American population was far greater than the population of England, for the government of America to continue to be administered in London.
John Ferling: Franklin thought America's population would surpass that of Great Britain by the middle of the 19th century, and he based his calculation on natural increase alone. When immigration is factored in, America was certain to have had a far larger population by 1850. I don't see how London could have avoided extending far greater autonomy to the Americans [over] the course of the 19th century.

What might have become of the 13 colonies post-war had Britain been victorious, as well as revolutionary leaders like George Washington?
Conway: Leaders of the rebellion might have been treated in the same manner as the leaders of the rebellion of 1745-6 in Scotland, who were executed for treason.
Ferling: If Franklin is to be believed, the British public was enraged toward the colonists at the time the war broke out; years of war only stoked those passions. Had the rebellion been crushed, retribution would have been the order of the day. Some leaders would have been executed, some imprisoned for long terms, and the colonists likely would have had to pay fines or faced some sort of economic punishment.

And what do you think would have happened to the rest of America – beyond the 13 colonies?
Ferling: The French Revolution might have been America's opening for attempting once again to gain independence. But assuming that had not been the case, I think London would have continued pushing towards the west. It almost certainly would have taken the British longer to reach the Pacific than it took the United States. British merchants looked askance at settlements beyond the Appalachian barrier, but Britain would have gotten there eventually.
Allison: Spain claimed the territory west of the Mississippi [River], but hardly controlled it. Britain probably would have kept the Native Americans of the Ohio Valley and the territory that is now Alabama and Mississippi, as they were trading partners. This might have stymied the spread of American settlers to the west. But it might not have, as the Royal Proclamation of 1763 had not done so.

The real impetus for American settlement of the Great Plains – the area between the Mississippi River and the Rocky Mountains, much of it wrested from Mexico in the [mid-19th century] – was to connect the east coast with the west. In the 1840s the United States and Britain nearly went to war over what is today British Columbia [in Canada]; '54°-40 or Fight' was James K Polk's campaign slogan in 1844 [before he became the 11th US president]. Britain, with its naval superiority, would have controlled the American west coast.

Spain would have been squeezed out. It's not clear if Mexico or the other Latin American countries would have developed in the same way had there not been an independent United States in North America.

What benefits – or disadvantages – might victory have brought Britain?
Conway: The benefits, if such they were, would have taken the form of greater economic control of the colonies, and especially of their overseas trade, which was subject to the restrictions of the 17th-century English Navigation Acts. But that advantage was unlikely to have been very much greater than the British reaped from defeat. The independent United States remained in a semi-colonial economic relationship with Britain

What if...
BRITAIN HAD WON THE WAR OF INDEPENDENCE?

" I don't see how London could have avoided extending far greater autonomy "

What if... BRITAIN HAD WON THE WAR OF INDEPENDENCE?

RIGHT
The Battle of Nassau was an American naval assault on the then British-ruled island in the Bahamas which took place in March 1776

for many years after 1783, consuming vast quantities of British manufactured goods and sending to Britain enormous quantities of raw materials. Had the British won the war, they would have been burdened by the costs of governing and defending America, so we can say that defeat left Britain with many of the benefits but few of the costs of empire.
Ferling: A great challenge would have been to somehow win back the hearts of the colonists. It would not have been easy. A victorious America largely hated the British for a century after the Revolution. Hatred would have lingered longer and burned more deeply in a defeated America.

How might nations, other than Britain and the US, have been affected if the war had gone the other way?
Allison: France, Spain and Native Americans [would have been] most notably [affected]. France supported the Americans, but primarily as a way to weaken Britain and protect France's West Indian colonies. Would the French Revolution have happened without the successful example of the American Revolution – or the huge debt France incurred by [participating in] it? Granted, France was reeling from an ineffective government overladen with aristocracy and political inefficiency, and the defeat in the Seven Years' War. Spain was fortifying its Mexican borders in the 1770s and 1780s; its main interest in the war in America was to get back Gibraltar.

The Native Americans were the big losers in the war though. The British were their allies, though allies the British sold out when it served their interests. I'm not singling out the British for doing this, as most nations tend to seek their own self-interest. The British had proposed an Indian buffer state in the Ohio Valley, and they were trading partners with the Iroquois, Creek and Cherokee tribes – one reason they supported the British rather than the Americans.

Could a one-nation unification with Canada have been on the cards for North America?
Conway: The Americans tried to conquer Canada in 1775, and wanted it ceded to the United States in the peace negotiations of 1782-3. But the British were determined to keep Canada, which was now increasingly gaining the Protestant population British governments had wanted since 1763, thanks to the exodus of American loyalists from the USA. If America had lost, then the loyalists may have stayed in the old British colonies, leaving Canada overwhelmingly francophone and Catholic, in which case it would have remained very different from the rest of the mainland British colonies.
Ferling: I think Britain would have opposed unification, at least for a long time after it crushed the American rebellion. During the Seven Years' War it had sought to keep the 13 colonies from unifying under one government, as Franklin had proposed in his Albany Plan of Union. Had it defeated the colonists in the Revolutionary War, Britain might have divided some colonies to keep them weak. The changes it sought to impose in Massachusetts' government in the Coercive Acts in 1775 probably would have been the rule of thumb in every colony.

Do you think Australia would have still

HOW WOULD IT BE DIFFERENT?

REAL TIMELINE

- **Intolerable Acts passed**
  The Intolerable, or Coercive, Acts are passed by the British government in early-1774 in response to the perceived lawlessness of the Boston Tea Party – a colonial uprising many years in the making.
  1774

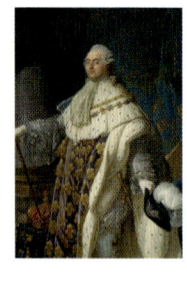

- **Continental Congress held**
  The First Continental Congress is formed and they agree to oppose the Intolerable Acts. From early on there's a sense that conflict is both inevitable and imminent.
  1774

- **War begins**
  The first shots are fired in the war, with the opening conflict at Lexington involving local Massachusetts militia (the formation of which had been suggested by the First Continental Congress in 1774) and British forces.
  19 April 1775

- **Battle of Bunker Hill**
  In this major battle, Patriot troops bravely resist a repeated British assault, only to be eventually worn down by the sheer numbers and persistence of the enemy – plus a lack of ammunition. The British lose massive numbers but prevail to take Bunker Hill.
  17 June 1775

- **Britain rejects peace**
  In the summer of 1775, King George III ignores the Second Continental Congress's Olive Branch Petition, and the war continues apace. In May 1776, King Louis XVI of France solves the Americans' munitions problem by granting a huge donation. Soon after the US Declaration of Independence is voted in on 4 July 1776.
  1775-1776

ALTERNATE TIMELINE

been developed as a penal colony if the 13 American colonies had remained under British control?

Conway: New South Wales in Australia was established as a penal colony, but if the North American colonies had remained British, there would have been less incentive to ship convicts so far. America was the cheaper option by a long way. Incidentally, the idea of imprisonment and reformation of convicts would have suffered a blow, as it was the end of transportation to the American colonies that provided an opportunity for reformers who argued that criminals should be incarcerated and improved, rather than executed or exported. More broadly, we can say that the loss of America saw a shift in British imperial focus towards the East – especially Asia. This so-called 'swing to the East' has perhaps been exaggerated, but there was undoubtedly a recalibration of imperial priorities. That said, expansion in India had already started, and would probably have continued, though not perhaps at the same pace.

Allison: Probably. Britain's real colonial interests in the 1770s were not America, but India, Jamaica and Barbados. And so Britain wanted control of sea routes to India, and also direct trade with China. Australia would be useful to both.

If Britain had retained control of America, how might this have impacted 20th-century events?

Conway: If we assume that the British had won the war, and the colonies had remained subject to the British crown, they would no doubt have entered World War I in the same manner as the British Dominions in 1914. Whether that would have tilted the balance in favour of the Allies and against Germany/Austria-Hungary is impossible to say; maybe a still-dependent America would not have industrialised so quickly and its population would have been smaller, with the result that the addition of strength was nowhere near as great as it was in 1917-18 [when they actually entered WWI].

Ferling: My understanding is that Britain made a concerted effort to smooth relations with the US beginning around 1890, which proved helpful during World War I. How that war would have been seen in an America that was tied to Britain as colonies or in a Commonwealth arrangement is difficult to know. Canada did not need any prodding to back London in 1914. However, there was a deep strain of resentment in America in 1776 (one can find it in Thomas Paine and Benjamin Franklin) at the colonies having been dragged repeatedly into that 'old rotten state's plundering wars' (Franklin). Such a sentiment might only have hardened over time and, as for many in Ireland, a European war might have been the spark for many Americans to rise up in favour of breaking away from Britain.

Canada
Canada's French Catholic influence remained strong and France threatened Britain with war, but lack of support and finance prevented this. Lower Canada, Upper Canada and most of America would likely unite into one legislative state.

The 13 British colonies
A heavy British military presence would have been necessary in the 13 colonies in order to retain control. The situation would have possibly resembled Northern Ireland, with violence and unrest – both political and social – never far away.

Native Americans
Native Americans would receive generous terms for allowing western expansion through their territory because of the overstretched British troops being unable to guard the east and conquer the west at the same time. Large areas of America remain firmly in tribal control well into the late-19th century.

Gun control
After defeating the rebels, American colonists would no longer be permitted to carry firearms, in an effort to try and 'de-claw' any separatist movements in areas like Boston and New England.

Southern states
The Southern colonies become more and more difficult to control due to the British abolition of slavery in 1833. Southern cotton lords fear for their livelihoods if their workforce is set free. Britain is forced to commit ever more troops and resources to guard its American colonies as the Southern states become more militant.

- **Washington for the win**
George Washington carries out a surprise attack on the British contingency at Trenton, NJ. The Patriots claim a decisive victory, boosting morale.
1776

- **British surrender**
The British army surrenders at Yorktown on 19 October 1781. In February of the following year, the British government decides to abandon the war.
1781-1782

- **Another war**
The USA declares war on Britain, reopening the conflict. The prior conflict has overshadowed the 1812 War, but *The Star-Spangled Banner* anthem dates from this time.
1812-1815

- **US enters WWI**
Having preferred a policy of neutrality, and with concern for trade with Britain in mind, America enters WWI, and US soldiers fight alongside the Brits.
April 1917

- **Battle of Long Island**
Sir William Howe, C-in-C of British forces, claims victory at Long Island. The Americans try to escape to Manhattan, but the British cut them off. George Washington is killed.
27 August 1776

- **Britain faces new enemy**
Support for America grows in Europe, particularly in France, and on 10 July 1778 France declares war on Britain. The French navy plays a key role.
1777-1778

- **Penal colonies**
The 13 American colonies along the Atlantic coast serve as the main destination for UK transportation. Far fewer convicts are sent to Australia.
1790

- **France invades Spain**
King Louis XVIII, angered by what was seen as Spain's gross betrayal in selling 'French' Louisiana, orders the invasion of Spain, but retreats when Britain weighs in.
1823

- **American population booms**
Controlled immigration into British North America has gradually increased, with transportation of criminals to both America and Australia ending in 1868.
1868

- **Anglo-American Agreement**
This pact officially ends the war. Patriot supporters who don't flee are imprisoned or hung, including key leaders like John Adams and Benjamin Franklin. Britain goes on to cement her hold of the colonies.
1776

- **Louisiana purchase**
With France effectively bankrupted by its support for the American Revolutionary War, Spain is courted by the British government and persuaded to release Louisiana. Britain purchases the territory at a discount.
1803

- **Act of union**
Lower Canada, Upper Canada and the American colonies are united into British North America. The British government appeases the French by granting trade with the regions that France had ceded.
1840-1867

What if...

ENTENTE HAD FORCED A WIN IN GALLIPOLI?

A devastating loss for the Ottoman Empire and the Central Powers could mean an early victory for Britain, France and Russia

INTERVIEW WITH
Professor William Philpott
Professor Philpott is Professor of the History of Warfare at King's College London, where he specialises in the history of the First World War and 20th Century Anglo-French relations.

What's the background to the Gallipoli campaign in 1914 and 1915?
Essentially what happens in 1914 is all military effort is committed by both sides to try and decide the war in Europe, but that stalemates towards the end of November, and the Turks join the war in early November 1914 on the side of the Central Powers. That in some ways distracts attention from the main theatre. Politicians looked outside for other strategic opportunities away from the Western Front, and they identify that they think Turkey is weak and vulnerable. The idea [for the Gallipoli campaign] is to connect the Western and Eastern allies, essentially to open up a sea route through the Dardanelles from the Mediterranean to Russia. So there's a clear strategic rationale behind the campaign. It's also rather rushed, it's driven by what Lord Kitchener at the time described as amateur strategists, politicians who come up with some bright ideas but don't really appreciate the practicalities of mounting military operations. Britain is seen as the driver of the campaign.

How did the campaign begin?
Over the winter of 1914, [the Allies] arrived by a complicated series of stages at a decision to mount a naval attack against the Dardanelles, believing that the Allied Anglo-based navy can force a passage up to Constantinople, which will topple the young Turk regime in the Ottoman Empire and lead to a relatively quick, bloodless victory in knocking Turkey quickly out of the war. It's not until after that naval operation is underway that they realise substantial troops are going to be required to make that campaign effective. The first idea is they'll need some troops to occupy Constantinople once the navy's got through, but when it's realised that the Turkish [defence] is strong, and the navy alone can't force a passage to the Dardanelles, they need an expeditionary force. The Mediterranean Expeditionary Force - a British, French coalition force - needs to actually land on the Gallipoli Peninsula to eliminate the defences, particularly artillery that's preventing the Allied ships advancing through the sea at Marmara up to Constantinople. That's the broad outline of the campaign.

How did the battle play out?
I think the Gallipoli Campaign was poorly managed. It was actually investigated after the war. Essentially what happens is that they mount this campaign by stages. They realise they're going to have to have an opposed landing on the Gallipoli Peninsula, which delays the first phase of the amphibious assault. It's not until 25 April [1915] that they actually manage to launch the amphibious operation against the Gallipoli Peninsula, by which time the Turkish defence is much better prepared than it would have been if they'd led the operation some weeks before. When the campaign stalemates into another trench-to-trench operation, then Kitchener has to send in piecemeal, small amounts of reinforcements [from India, New Zealand, and Australia in 1915]. Again it stalemates in the face of a consolidated Turkish defence, and they mount one final large operation in the middle of August to try and push forward at the Suvla Bay beachhead. But that makes no progress and thereafter they start to realise that the campaign is not going anywhere. But again, there's a series of stages before

RIGHT
New Zealand troops land at Anzac Cove

What if...
ENTENTE HAD FORCED A WIN IN GALLIPOLI?

What if... ENTENTE HAD FORCED A WIN IN GALLIPOLI?

they finally do make the decision to evacuate towards the end of 1915. They learnt a lot from this experience about how better to plan, direct and organise military operations.

What were the major outcomes of the campaign?
The outcome for the Allies was a humiliation. They failed in their objective to get through to support the Russians. They had the embarrassment of having to evacuate their troops, [and] they needed to reinforce the defence of Egypt, which was now under threat from Turkish advances. In some ways, Britain was trying to run a colonial-style campaign, whereas this required more modern methods of military management and administration. The Turks got a national victory, whereas they weren't doing particularly well on other fronts, and they ended up doing well against the Russians in the Caucasus. But in some ways the real bonus in Turkey was that it removed the threat to Constantinople, the centre of the Ottoman Empire. The campaigns that the Allies were mounting against Turkey thereafter, although they were more effective in the second half of the war, in Palestine for example, and later again in Mesopotamia, they were a long way from the Turkish heartlands and in some ways it guaranteed Turkish security. It was really the clash of Bulgaria in 1918 that opened up a land route for the Allies to attack Constantinople again. That really convinced Turkey that they were losing the war and should seek an armistice with the Allies in September and October 1918.

Is there a scenario where the Allies win the Battle of Gallipoli?
If the naval attack had been effective in March [1915], that would have really changed the nature of the war. The expectation was if Allied ships appeared at Constantinople, the Turkish government would collapse and a peace party would come to power and take Turkey out of the war. That's possibly quite a naive expectation but if it had happened of course it would have really changed the complexion of the war in early 1915. It would have removed one of Germany's major allies, and it would have probably dissuaded Bulgaria from joining the war on the Central Powers' side in September [1915], which in some ways was the factor that compromised the Allied positions on the Gallipoli Peninsula. It obliged Kitchener and others to take the decision to withdraw.

What would have happened if the Allies had won?
If the Turkish state had collapsed, I think you would have seen an attempt to incorporate large parts of Turkish territory into various European states and empires.

ABOVE LEFT
There were heavy casualties on both sides, with more than 300,000 deaths in all

RIGHT
Had the Gallipoli campaign succeeded, the US might not have entered the war

BOTTOM RIGHT
Australia and New Zealand remember the event every year on Anzac Day, 25 April

One of the diplomatic agreements, before the campaign was launched, between Russia and her allies was that Russia at the end of the war would have control of Constantinople and the straits. This was something that Britain and France had opposed for the best part of a century, so there were some clear changes in geopolitical alignments. But what you'd also have seen was the breaking up of the rest of the Ottoman Empire into different colonial spheres of influence or formal colonies, roughly along the lines of what you would see in 1918.

What were the goals of the Allies at time of the Gallipoli campaign?
I think the mindset of 1915 was to break up the Turkish Empire and incorporate it into the European empires that had been growing throughout the 19th century. Things change by 1917, of course, when you get Woodrow Wilson in America coming into the war. And so the settlement you get in 1918 and 1919 is very much a watered-down version of perhaps the plan that was drawn up by the pragmatic diplomats of imperialist Europe in 1915. You get mandates in some of these areas and these nations, you get the Turks essentially fighting a war of national

> "The mindset of the Allies in 1915 was to break up the Turkish Empire"

The horrors of Gallipoli

Many soldiers involved in the Allied campaign in Gallipoli considered it to be one of the worst fronts of the war, not so much because of the brutality of the fighting, but for the awful conditions that they had to live and fight under. Bodies left in no man's land, lice infestations, dysentery outbreaks and more made day-to-day life on this front a constant nightmare, with the potential for disease being an ever-present worry. In these respects conditions in Turkey were not so different from those of the Western Front in Europe, but the added pressures of the heat and a lack of water made life even more uncomfortable. Maintaining your strength in such circumstances, not to mention general morale, would have been nearly impossible, which likely contributed to how Allied forces performed on this front.

A field surgeon attempts to work on an injured soldier in the Dardanelles, 1915

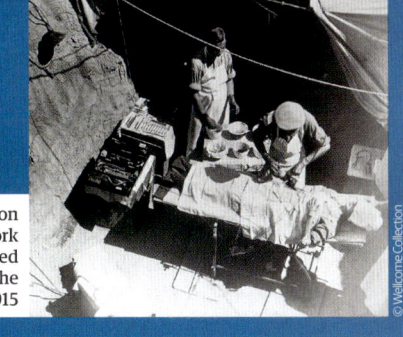

independence to sustain and develop what is now the modern Turkish secular state.

Would an Allied victory at Gallipoli have brought World War I to a close sooner?

I think it would. Simply [because] it would have altered the balance of power in the Balkans; it would have given the Allies freedom to use the large number of forces that were tied down in the Middle Eastern war more effectively in Europe either for landing in the Balkans, supporting Serbia, or having more forces to engage Germany on the Western Front. The German position would have been more difficult and potentially the war would have ended earlier, but there would still have been a long, hard war to fight against Germany, Austria, and Hungary before that outcome would be decided. So yes, victory at Gallipoli would make the Allies' task easier. They'll have two enemies to defeat rather than four, but it will still be a difficult task and the effort and sacrifice would still characterise the First World War. It might have ended in 1917, which would have changed the geopolitical situation, if Russia hadn't collapsed [and] if America hadn't mobilised and joined the war. We would live in a very different world to the one we do today.

What if...

THE US HAD STAYED OUT OF THE GREAT WAR?

A prolonged conflict, a modified Treaty of Versailles and no League of Nations may have transpired without direct American involvement

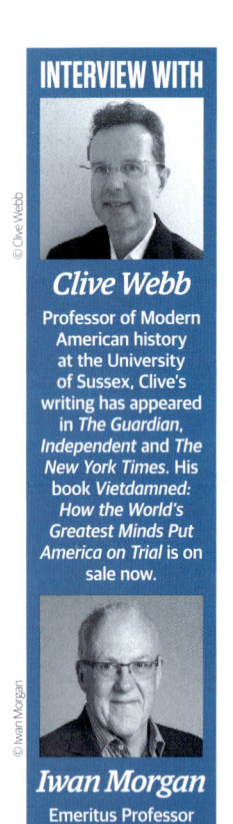

INTERVIEW WITH

Clive Webb
Professor of Modern American history at the University of Sussex, Clive's writing has appeared in *The Guardian*, *Independent* and *The New York Times*. His book *Vietdamned: How the World's Greatest Minds Put America on Trial* is on sale now.

Iwan Morgan
Emeritus Professor of US Studies at the Institute of the Americas, University College London, and an honorary fellow of Oxford University's Rothermere American Institute, Iwan has authored many books on US presidents, including *FDR: Transforming the Presidency and Renewing America*.

RIGHT
US General John J Pershing arrives in France, 3 June 1917

Although the United States had supported the Allied cause in the First World War with weapons, supplies and financial considerations, the introduction of American troops and other military assets in a direct role in 1917-18 was welcomed by the war-weary nations of Britain and France, and was an ominous development for Germany and the Central Powers. However, the absence of this US commitment to an active military role in the Great War may well have altered the outcome of the conflict along with the structure and steadiness of the tenuous peace that followed the armistice and the terms of the Treaty of Versailles.

How would the outcome of the Great War have been altered if the US had not entered the fight?

Clive Webb: Historians are not usually in the prediction business, not least when it concerns a future that never came to pass, and that may account for the lack of consensus about how US neutrality would have affected the outcome of the war. Some alternative histories have the Central Powers claiming victory. That would have led to Germany dictating peace terms that established it as the hegemonic power in Europe. Britain and France would've been ruined economically and unable to pay their debts, which in turn would've had ruinous consequences for their US creditors.

Others insist that the Allies would eventually have won. At least one historian has claimed that it would have been better for the USA not to intervene because the mobilisation of the American Expeditionary Forces (AEF) expended time, effort and resources that should have been invested in the British and French military. The USA therefore slowed rather than accelerated Allied victory. In a history where Britain and France used their unrestricted access to US war production to overcome the Central Powers, they would have no need to invite US President Woodrow Wilson to the peace table and could have imposed more punitive terms on their defeated foe. That settlement would have restored the same international system that had led to war in the first place.

My approach is to work backwards from what we know. US intervention raised Allied morale at a crucial moment in the war when Britain and France had suffered huge losses without approaching a decisive breakthrough. They were more or less financially bankrupt and unable to pay for further resources from the US. There was therefore little prospect of complete victory over the Central Powers without American support either in terms of industrial production or military reinforcement. So US intervention was crucial both to when and on what terms the war finally ended.

Had either side won without the USA having intervened, then Wilson would not have been involved in post-war negotiations. That would have meant an abandonment of his aspirations for a new international order based on collective security and free trade. The League of Nations would not have been created.

Iwan Morgan: The odds still favoured an Allied victory. The Allied blockade was taking its toll on the German home front, Germany had not been able to rapidly transfer sufficient units from the Eastern Front, and the establishment of a unified Anglo-French command made for improved defensive and offensive operations in 1918. That said, the Germans may have continued the war longer than they did, leading to overwhelming war weariness among the British and French, but there was also the question of how long Germany could have gone on fighting.

Would the German 1918 Spring Offensive still have taken place?

Webb: Germany would certainly have had more time to prepare the Spring Offensive if it had not been rushed into action by US intervention. Whether that could have proven decisive in securing victory depends on how well prepared and executed the offensive was. It is

What if...
THE US HAD STAYED OUT OF THE GREAT WAR?

"The odds still favoured an Allied victory"

What if... THE US HAD STAYED OUT OF THE GREAT WAR?

THE PAST

1918
SPRING OFFENSIVE SPUTTERS
The German Spring Offensive of 1918 shocked the Allies and made initial territorial gains. However, lack of resources, including troops, weapons and equipment, rendered the offensive unsustainable as British and French resistance stiffened along the length of the Western Front penetration. As well as exhaustion of troops, the Germans had logistical challenges and overextended supply lines. Allied counterattacks were bolstered with the expectation and continuing arrival of American troops in Europe. Meanwhile, economic unrest and war fatigue in Germany served to destabilise the situation at home, contributing to the necessity of a negotiated peace.

1917
AMERICAN TROOPS ARRIVE
The first American ground troops arrived in Europe in June 1917, but did not fight on the frontline until the October. They underwent extensive training after reaching France, and controversy developed as to their actual deployment to the front. While British and French officers proposed that American troops fall under their command as replacements, General John J Pershing insisted that US forces would serve under American officers. US soldiers used French and British weapons and equipment regularly.

1918
ONE HUNDRED DAYS
A series of Allied counterattacks in response to the German Spring Offensive of 1918 led to the rapid exhaustion of the German capability to continue the war. The Allies' Hundred Days Offensive began on 8 August 1918, and drove the enemy out of France and beyond its fortifications of the Hindenburg Line. Allied commanders, including British, French and US officers, had conceived the Hundred Days to seize the initiative in the field; the Germans had suffered extensive casualties in earlier fighting and become overextended, unable to hold their spring gains. By 11 November 1918, the armistice was concluded as Germany had no viable alternative other than to seek peace.

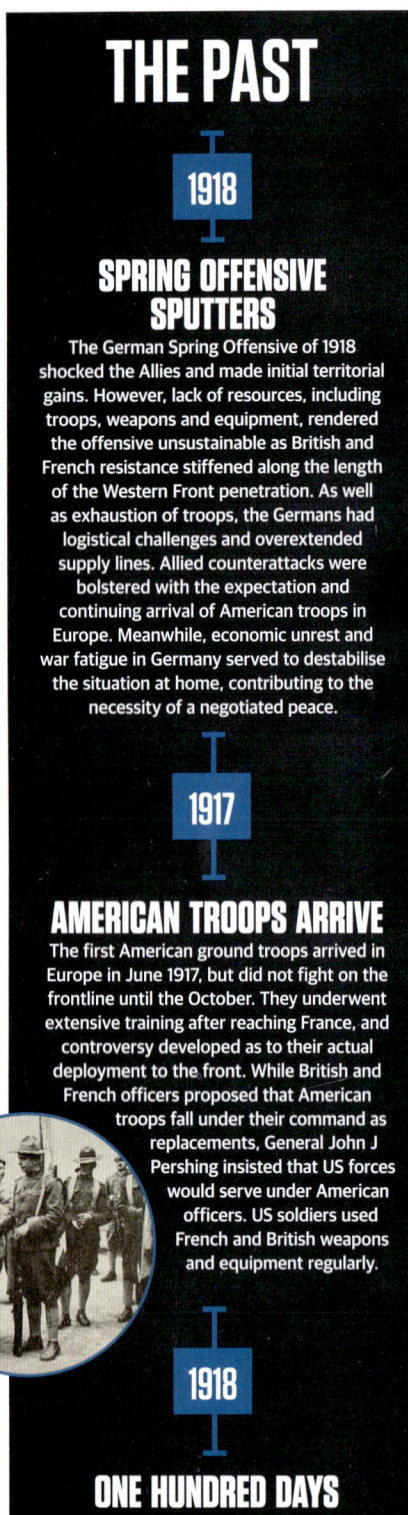

ABOVE Two American soldiers rush towards a German bunker

BELOW Allied artillery crews head to the frontline

RIGHT British and French soldiers march through a town, spring 1918

plausible that without the US entering the war Germany would have been able to counter the Allies long enough to secure a negotiated peace settlement that would have avoided the anger and bitterness which fuelled Nazism.

Morgan: True, but Germany's own need to end the war as soon as possible also drove the offensive, which petered out before large numbers of American troops arrived. Economically, the British and French were more capable of continuing the war than the Germans.

Would a more balanced armistice have been possible?
Morgan: The Kaiser's position would still have been in doubt had the Entente triumphed without US involvement because it blamed German militarism for the war. Arguably Wilson wanted to be a moderating influence at Versailles, but the French wanted a harsh peace and the British by and large supported them. Without the US at the table, the Germans may well have got worse terms.

Would Germany still have been defeated without the Americans?
Webb: Had the lack of US intervention led to a military stalemate then a more balanced armistice is conceivable. What the terms of the settlement would have been is open to speculation but presumably would mean the Germans retained more of their territories and industrial base, and also not have to concede entire blame for causing the war.

How would the Entente fare without the billions of dollars in loans from the United States?
Webb: Had America maintained the strictest neutrality and not provided loans to Britain and France they could not have won the war. Without either the will or the way to fight on probably into 1919, stalemate or defeat was the only conceivable outcome.

Morgan: The Entente had already borrowed heavily from US creditors long before the US entered the war. Whether the flow of credit would have continued if the war had gone deep into a fifth or sixth year is a matter of debate, but US financiers were so heavily invested in an Anglo-French victory that they could not easily have stopped the loan spigot.

Would the 'American Century' have been cancelled?
Webb: The United States was the most powerful industrial nation in the world by the time of the Great War. Its rise as the preeminent global superpower would have occurred with or without the conflict. The US retreated into isolationism in reaction to a war that many Americans believed they should never have become involved in and,

of course, the country did not become a member of the League of Nations. In that sense, the conflict slowed rather than advanced the international dominance of the US.

Morgan: The 'American Century' would have happened anyway because the longer the war went on the greater would have been the depletion of the resources of the once-Great Powers of Europe.

How would not entering the war have affected US history?

Webb: Not entering the war would have affected the course of US history both domestically and internationally. The war had an important impact on US race and gender relations. War production accelerated the migration of African-Americans from the rural South to the industrial North. The experience of serving in a segregated army also sharpened Black political consciousness. Black soldiers realised they would not benefit from the war they were fighting in, the democratic rhetoric of the US government meaning little for them in reality. This led many Black veterans to become more involved in the fight for racial equality after the war. US intervention accelerated the momentum of the civil rights struggle, which would conceivably have been slower had the country remained neutral. A similar case can be made about women's rights because the important contribution of women to the American war effort converted Wilson to the cause of female suffrage.

ABOVE
Generals Paul von Hindenburg and Erich Ludendorff discuss German strategy during WWI

Neutrality would not have immunised the United States from the influenza pandemic, but the scale and speed of infection owed much to the war. The first documented case of 'Spanish' flu occurred at an army base in Kansas and the concentration of soldiers in unsanitary conditions acted as an incubator of the disease. And it was veterans returning from overseas who were responsible for the second wave of the virus reaching the United States. There is no way to calculate how many fewer Americans would have died than the 675,000 who actually lost their lives to the disease.

The forces that caused or deepened the Great Depression - the destabilisation of the international economic system, countries defaulting on loans, tariff wars, inadequate business and banking deregulation - would all be in play whether or not the USA had intervened in the First World War.

Morgan: The 'Spanish' flu was completely misnamed. It arguably began in the United States and was transported to Europe by the AEF. It may not have had such devastating consequences on the rest of the world if the US had not entered the war, but America's international connections may still have spread it far and wide.

The catastrophic effect of the Great War on the European economies made an international economic crisis almost inevitable. An Anglo-French victory would still have imposed harsh reparation terms on Germany, with the strong likelihood of a financial crisis occurring once nations sought to reestablish the gold standard. Without US involvement in the Great War, there may well have been an effort to create some form of collective security, but it would have depended on Anglo-French will to enforce it - so its duration would have been limited.

THE POSSIBILITY

1917

AMERICAN ISOLATIONISM

Woodrow Wilson won re-election in 1916 with the slogan: "He Kept Us Out Of War." During the campaign, he was aware of the reluctance of the people to enter a 'European War', but the sinking of the RMS Lusitania, the declaration of unrestricted submarine warfare, the revelation of the 1917 Zimmermann Telegram and other German provocations swayed American public opinion, and Wilson went to Congress for a declaration of war in April 1917. Had US Isolationists been more forceful in their opposition or German hostility better contained, the situation on the battlefields of Europe would have been altered.

1918

KAISER WILHELM II REMAINS IN POWER

Continued US neutrality in the war might have allowed Kaiser Wilhelm II to remain in power. He abdicated his throne and fled to the Netherlands on 9 November 1918, two days before the conclusion of the armistice. He had lost the support of the military, and civil unrest was fomenting in the streets due to war weariness and prolonged economic hardship. His removal from power would facilitate peace negotiations with the Allies since the kaiser had long presented an antagonistic posture, while Germany sought territorial gains and international prestige prior to the outbreak of hostilities.

1920

RISE OF NAZIS PREVENTED

Had prolonged US neutrality allowed Germany to prevail in the war or achieve a more favourable negotiated peace than the terms forced upon the nation with the Treaty of Versailles, the rise of right-wing totalitarian political and paramilitary forces in post-war Germany could have been curbed or eliminated. Economic collapse may have been inevitable due to the cost of the war, but the Nazis and their trumpeting of the 'stab in the back' theory would likely have been implausible in the minds of many Germans. In actuality, the Nazis were successful in quashing moderate and left-wing opposition, while asserting that the German military had not been defeated in the field but betrayed by subversive elements at home.

What if...
Book of Alternative Military History

Future PLC Quay House, The Ambury, Bath, BA1 1UA

Bookazine Editorial
Group Editor **Sarah Bankes**
Senior Designer **Harriet Knight**
Head of Art & Design **Greg Whitaker**
Editorial Director **Jon White**
Managing Director **Grainne McKenna**

All About History Editorial
Editor **Jonathan Gordon**
Art Editor **Kym Winters**
Editor in Chief **Tim Williamson**
Senior Art Editor **Duncan Crook**

Cover images
Sara Biddle, Getty Images, Alamy

Photography
All copyrights and trademarks are recognised and respected

Advertising
Media packs are available on request
Commercial Director **Clare Dove**

International
Head of Print Licensing **Rachel Shaw**
licensing@futurenet.com
www.futurecontenthub.com

Circulation
Head of Newstrade **Tim Mathers**

Production
Head of Production **Mark Constance**
Production Project Manager **Matthew Eglinton**
Advertising Production Manager **Joanne Crosby**
Digital Editions Controller **Jason Hudson**
Production Managers **Keely Miller, Nola Cokely, Vivienne Calvert, Fran Twentyman**

Printed in the UK

Distributed by Marketforce – www.marketforce.co.uk
For enquiries, please email: mfcommunications@futurenet.com

GPSR EU RP (for authorities only)
eucomply OÜ Pärnu mnt 139b-14 11317, Tallinn, Estonia
hello@eucompliancepartner.com, +3375690241

What if... Book of Alternative Military History (AHB6997)
© 2025 Future Publishing Limited

We are committed to only using magazine paper which is derived from responsibly managed, certified forestry and chlorine-free manufacture. The paper in this bookazine was sourced and produced from sustainable managed forests, conforming to strict environmental and socioeconomic standards.

All contents © 2025 Future Publishing Limited or published under licence. All rights reserved. No part of this magazine may be used, stored, transmitted or reproduced in any way without the prior written permission of the publisher. Future Publishing Limited (company number 2008885) is registered in England and Wales. Registered office: Quay House, The Ambury, Bath BA1 1UA. All information contained in this publication is for information only and is, as far as we are aware, correct at the time of going to press. Future cannot accept any responsibility for errors or inaccuracies in such information. You are advised to contact manufacturers and retailers directly with regard to the price of products/services referred to in this publication. Apps and websites mentioned in this publication are not under our control. We are not responsible for their contents or any other changes or updates to them. This magazine is fully independent and not affiliated in any way with the companies mentioned herein.

FUTURE Connectors. Creators. Experience Makers.

Future plc is a public company quoted on the London Stock Exchange (symbol: FUTR)
www.futureplc.com

Chief Executive Officer **Jon Steinberg**
Non-Executive Chairman **Richard Huntingford**
Chief Financial Officer **Sharjeel Suleman**

Tel +44 (0)1225 442 244

Part of the

ALL ABOUT HISTORY
bookazine series